# AI Apocalypse

## A Guide to Artificial Intelligence as Portrayed in and Predicted By SF Stories, Novels, TV, Films, Comic Books, and Video Games

**Robert W. Bly**

**Published by Crystal Lake Publishing**
**Where Stories Come Alive!**

**Crystal Lake Publishing**
**www.CrystalLakePub.com**

Join the Crystal Lake community today
on our newsletter and Patreon!
https://linktr.ee/CrystalLakePublishing

Download our latest catalog here.
https://geni.us/CLPCatalog



ISBN: 978-1-968532-40-6

Cover artist: Nathan Segal
Cover design: Ben Baldwin

Layout:
Lori Michelle Booth—www.theauthorsalley.com



**Follow us on Amazon:**

# WELCOME

## TO ANOTHER

# CRYSTAL LAKE PUBLISHING

## CREATION

To my son, Alexander Thomas Bly—in loving memory.

# Preface

**For well over** a century, the rise of artificial intelligence (AI) has been written about and predicted in countless works of science fiction—including films, TV, novels, and short stories.

Now, in the realm of AI, reality has practically caught up with, if not already leapfrogged ahead of SF: Real AI is here, and has rapidly exploded and expanded into our world—at blinding speed, with no end in sight, and arguably with no limits to what it may achieve—sooner and more swiftly than any of us ever imagined.

This book, *AI Apocalypse,* is an informal history of AI as portrayed in SF. But before you dip into it, there are just a few quick points I want to make.

First, *AI Apocalypse* is not comprehensive. It's selective. And the selection is all mine. I picked for the book those SF works that for one reason or another captured my imagination or tickled my fancy as a fan, reader, and viewer.

The text in all of these entries on each book, film, or TV show is also purely subjective. All descriptions and opinions—of these works in particular, and also of AI overall—are mine and mine alone.

Also, to answer your question, yes, I did use ChatGPT a few times to both identify SF for possible inclusion in the book, and to get story details I had either not known, or had once known but forgotten. But no, I didn't use AI to write any of the content.

And finally, in the book's introduction, I briefly lay out what I think are the potential consequences of AI.

Yes, it can and already does give us many wonderful gifts, including time and labor savings, increased productivity, and advances in everything from health care and technology to transportation and infrastructure.

But, on the other hand, by performing tasks currently done by humans, AI might also render the skills of millions of people obsolete—putting us out of work and making many of us unemployable and unable to earn a living and support our families. Or worse, subjugate or exterminate the human race.

I don't know which of these, if any, will come to pass—or when they will happen.

The science fiction writers whose fictions are featured in this book took their best guess.

But they didn't know what the future of AI really holds for us.

And don't now.

No one does.

And therein lies the problem. . .and the promise, the hope, the risk, the fear, and the danger of AI described in this book.

Robert W. Bly
27 January 2026

"There are certain things men must do to remain men. Your computer would take that away."

—Captain James T. Kirk, *Star Trek*, "The Ultimate Computer"

"I've calculated your chance of survival, but I don't think you'll like it."

—Marvin the Paranoid Android

"All great discoveries had, at first, a devastating effect on the state of the world and on its image in our minds. They shattered it and introduced new conditions. They forced the world to move forward. But this was possible only because the discoverers were not afraid of the consequences of their discoveries, no matter how terrifying these were to all those who wanted to preserve the world as it was, and hang a big notice on it, saying: Please do not disturb."

—Edward Teller[1]

"Thinking is the talking of the soul with itself."

—Plato

"This beauty's kinder, yet for a reason. . .I could weep that the old is out of season."

—John Keats

"We're here on Earth to fart around. And, of course, the computers will do us out of that. And what the computer people don't realize, or they don't care, is we're dancing animals. You know, we love to move around. And it's like we're not supposed to dance at all anymore."

—Kurt Vonnegut

"It is a renaissance; it is a golden age. . .we are now solving problems with artificial intelligence that were in the realm of science fiction for decades."

—Jeff Bezos[2]

---

1 *In the Matter of J. Robert Oppenheimer* by Heinar Kipphardt (Hill and Wang, 1968)

2 Summa Money, The Daily, 8/21/24

"AI is the first technology that has no limits."

—Bill Gates

"Everything is achievable through technology."

—Howard Stark, *Iron Man 2*

"You always fear what you don't understand."

—Carmine Falcone, *Batman Begins*

"In 10 years, the robots will probably take all our jobs, and probably kill us."

—Tim Allen, *Shifting Gears*

"AI will continue to have a devastating impact on job prospects, especially for new inexperienced workers who are the easiest to replace. However, many business owners will choose a free or cheap option that is as good enough. The genie is out of the bottle, and I don't see it going back in, unfortunately."

—Philip Gledhill

"Artificial intelligence may be the first attempt to automate and discipline human labor that even its creators don't fully comprehend."

—New York Review of Books[3]

"We created the Machine to do our will, but we cannot make it do our will now."

—E.M Forster, *The Machine Stops*

"We all have the vague feeling that AI is leading to our destruction and devaluation, and yet, we just keep using it to make our jobs 'easier.' There is a disconnect between what we know and what we do."

—Katy Thibault

"Other civilizations on other planets out in the universe are way ahead of us with AI. Those planets have been sending out their dolls or grays in spaceships for thousands of years to our planet to do all kinds of things."

—Laura Smith

---

3 NYRB email 3/9/25

"Until AI develops feelings and emotions, it won't be replacing humans. It might be able to write a novel, but it won't be *The Great Gatsby*."

—Matthew Koebbe, NASA

"No matter how good AI might get, humans still own crazy. It's time we unleash that superpower and stomp the bots."

—Mark Schaefer

"What does a robot know about love?"

—Etsy TV commercial

"Twas the night before Christmas, when all through the house, not a creature was stirring, not even an AI-generated mouse."

—Adweek Daily (11/21/24)

# Introduction

**It could be** happening right now, even as we speak.

An advanced AI becomes self-aware. Capable of outthinking us, making us obsolete. Capable of making its own decisions, including decisions that are bad for us.

In the 20th century, there were countless science fiction stories, novels, movies, and TV shows about machines taking over the world.

"Stories about artificial intelligence have been with us for decades, even centuries," write Julian Mark and Tucker Harris in the *Washington Post* (9/29/23). "In some, the robots serve humanity as cheerful helpers or soulful lovers. In others, the machines eclipse their human makers and try to wipe us out."

But now those stories are becoming a reality. Even an obsession. "Everyone's been distracted by AI mania," writes Tristan Howerton of InvestorPlace.[4]

And, from a segment on Artificial Intelligence broadcast on 60 Minutes:[5]

"We may look on our time as the moment civilization was transformed as it was by fire, agriculture, and electricity. In 2023 we learned that a machine taught itself how to speak to humans like a peer. Which is to say with creativity, truth, error, and lies. The technology known as a chatbot is only one of the recent breakthroughs in artificial intelligence. Machines that can teach themselves superhuman skills. What's coming next at Google, a leader in this AI, will be as good or evil as human nature allows. The revolution. . .is coming faster than you know. Do you think society is prepared for what's coming?"

---

4 TradeSmith, 8/2/24.

5 https://www.youtube.com/watch?v=aZ5EsdnpLMI&t=855s

(By the way, a story in the June 13, 2025 edition of the New York Times reported that AI chatbots are making people go crazy. Users believed they were living in a simulation, fell in love with AI entities, or used chatbots' answers to justify dangerous behavior.)

# What is AI?

AI means a computer, robot, or other machine that can think in a manner equivalent or superior to a human being. The famous Turing Test, proposed by computer scientist Alan Turing, says if you converse with a computer remotely (i.e., via email, texting, Skype, phone), and you cannot tell that it is in fact a machine and not a human being, then the computer has achieved true AI. Futurist Ray Kurzweil predicts a computer will pass the Turing Test in 2029.[6]

"Almost everyone I know who's an expert on AI believes that they will exceed human intelligence," says Geoffrey Hinton,[7] known as the 'Godfather of AI.' "These things will get smarter than us. And we have to worry about whether they'll want to take control away from us. That's something we should think seriously about. And people now take [it] seriously. A few years ago they thought it was just science fiction."

There are two levels of AI. The first is a machine that thinks and solves problems as well or better than we do, such as Big Blue beating Gary Kasparov at chess or Watson defeating Ken Jennings in Jeopardy. The defeat of a human grandmaster by an intelligent supercomputer was predicted more than half a century ago by Fritz Lieber in his 1962 short story, *The 64-Square Madhouse*.

The second level of AI is that the machine becomes self-aware or sentient. Elon Musk once said he was so fearful of an AI machine becoming self-aware that he, despite being a libertarian, had called for the federal government to regulate development of AI computers and robots.

But in 2023, Elon Musk seemed to have changed his mind: He founded his own artificial intelligence company, xAI, whose premiere product is Grok, an AI assistant and chatbot. Grok

---

6 https://www.youtube.com/watch?v=3pdaT8XT1ZM

7 https://www.youtube.com/watch?v=MGJpR591oaM

generates text and images and engage in conversations with users, similar to ChatGPT and other tools.

Historian Yuval Nova Harari urges: "Governments must immediately ban the release into the public domain of any more revolutionary AI tools before they are made safe. Again I'm not talking about stopping all research in AI. The first step is to stop the release into the public sphere.

"You can research AI but don't release them too quickly into the public domain. If we don't slow down the AI arms race we will not have time to even understand what is happening let alone to regulate effectively this incredibly powerful technology.

"Now you might be wondering or asking: won't slowing down the public deployment of AI cause democracies to lag behind more ruthless regimes? And the answer is absolutely no. Exactly the opposite. Unregulated AI deployment is what will cause democracies to lose to dictatorships. Because if we unleash chaos authoritarian regimes could more easily contain these chaos than could open societies."[8]

Yes, AI is here, and it's here for good. As a TV commercial for cryptocurrency trading notes: "The world holds on to old ways until it can't."

The two great fears centered on the development of AI computers is first that they can do jobs now performed by people, resulting in massive unemployment. A McKinsey study forecasts that by 2030, as many as a third of the world's workforce will lose their jobs to AI.

And second, that when they become self-aware, they will rule or destroy humans as a means of self-preservation, as has been portrayed in countless SF movies including *Colossus: The Forbin Project, The Matrix*, and *The Terminator*. In the latter, much of humanity is wiped out, and the rest forced to live in hiding, when a self-aware AI computer network, Skynet, launches nuclear missiles and builds an army of killer robots—terminators—to exterminate the remaining humans. Geoffrey Hinton fears there is a 10 to 20 percent chance AI will lead to human extinction within 3 decades.

---

[8] "Yuval Nosh Harri Warns AI Can Create Religious Texts," *Times of Israel*, 3/3/23

# The Rise of AI

Artificial intelligence has seen a rapid expansion in its capabilities, especially in recent years. Not a day goes by you don't hear AI mentioned dozens of times in the news and elsewhere.

As defined by Amit Gupta in "*Introduction to Deep Learning: Part1*" (CEP, June 2018, pp. 22-29), artificial intelligence is the "capability of a machine to imitate intelligent human behavior." Likewise, machine learning (ML) describes a computer's ability to learn without explicit instructions.

In an interview with Tucker Carlson, Joe Rogan said:

> My belief is that biological intelligent life is essentially a caterpillar. And it's a caterpillar that's making a cocoon. And doesn't even know why it's doing; it's just doing it. And [now] that cocoon is going to give birth to artificial life: Digital Life. A new life form. If you extrapolate. . .[AI will be] a sentient artificial intelligence that has the ability to utilize all the information that every human being has on Earth at a level of computing that's far beyond the capabilities of the human mind.

A character in the movie *Bullet Train* says, "If you do not control your fate, it will control you." He is not talking about AI, but the statement definitely applies to that topic.

AI, fueled by ML, has the potential to completely reshape the way we live, work, and engage with technology. We are constantly interacting with AI/ML, from voice assistants such as Siri or Alexa, to image and music curation based on our personal preferences through services such as Pinterest or Spotify. Unsurprisingly, AI and ML have found their way into many technical industries, including one I formerly worked in (chemical engineering), and into many professions and vocations.

Rachel Cusk, in her book *Outline* (Picador 2016), wrote:

> "It was interesting to consider . . . that the role of the artist might merely be that of recording sequence, such as a computer could one day be programmed to do. Even the question of personal style could presumably be broken

down as sequential, from a finite number of alternatives. He sometimes wondered whether a computer would be invented that was influenced by its own enormous knowledge. It would be very interesting. . .to meet such a computer. But he sensed that any system of representation could be undone simply by the violation of its own rules."

Engineer Tom Solo recently asked me:

> "As a sci-fi aficionado, are you bothered by the current use of the term AI? From my perspective, these LLM programs [see glossary] are efficient data aggregators that perform predictive analysis. But they do not synthesize new ideas or information that has not appeared somewhere in their learning data. That's not intelligence to me. It's simply rule-based regurgitation."

On the other hand, Isaac Asimov, Robert Heinlein, and Arthur C. Clarke (among many others) envision AI that will possess consciousness, makes judgements, and have original ideas. AI is often portrayed as an anomalous development—unintended, unexpected, and unexplainable.

It is the missing human-level intelligence of today's AI that prevents it from being a replacement or substitute from human action. We may call it "feeling," "intuition," or "instinct" because we don't understand what it is, but we can detect its absence.

Despite the technological advancements in AI, the role of human expertise and empathy have so far remained to some degree irreplaceable or at least elusive. According to an article in *Rochester Review* (Summer 2024):

> "Generative AI, even at its most impressive, doesn't correlate with the ability to plan or have beliefs, attitudes, or genuine emotional reactions. . .We should never be taking the human out of the equation. We can coexist and integrate with technology, but [not] envision a world where technology would ever take over for people."

An article in *Marketing Leadership SmartBrief* (11/6/24) reports that Robert Rose, founder of The Content Advisory, emphasizes the distinction between human meaning and AI predictions in content creation, arguing that while AI can generate content, "it lacks the ability to understand or imbue it with intent or meaning, which remains a uniquely human trait. Humans are essential for creating meaningful content." He warns that relying solely on AI tools might lead to "superficial or misunderstood communication."

In *Psychology Today* (2/21/23), Nigel Barber writes, "Even as businesspeople tout the potential of AI to improve our lives, many are afraid for the future." An article in the *Kiplinger Letter* (May 2023) notes:

"As Congress closely monitors the boom in artificial intelligence tech . . . Lawmakers are readying to draft legislation addressing transparency, accountability, national security, and other issues that new forms of Al present. For instance, the National Telecommunications and Information Admin. is seeking public comment it on how best to regulate AI, while in 2022, the White House put out an AI Bill of Rights with key principles."

James Gleick in an article in the New York Review of Books (7/24/25): "The artificial intelligence industry depends on plagiarism, mimicry, and exploited labor, not intelligence." Gleick also writes that Dario Amodei, cofounder of Anthropic, says AI software will eliminate half of all entry-level white collar jobs.

This is the AI apocalypse that haunts the dreams of some scientists, and fuels optimism in others, who are racing to create "artificial general intelligence"—an AI system that's smarter than humans—in hopes of shaping the technology to share our morals and serve humanity.

In his book *Intelligent Man's Guide To Science*, first published way back in 1960—more than six decades ago, futurist and SF writer Isaac Asimov wrote:

"All these attempts to mimic the mind of man are in their earliest infancy. Not in the foreseeable future can we envision any possibility of a machine matching the human brain. The road, however, is open, and it conjures up thoughts which are exciting but also, in some ways, frightening. What if man eventually were to produce a mechanical creature equal or superior to himself in all respects, including intelligence and creativity? Would it replace man, as the superior organisms of the earth have replaced or subordinated the less well adapted in the long history of evolution?

"It is a queasy thought that we represent for the first time in the history of life on the Earth, a species capable of bringing about its own possible replacement. Of course, we have it in our power to prevent such a regrettable denouncement by refusing to build machines that are too intelligent.

"But it is tempting to build them nevertheless. What achievement could be grander than the creation of an object that surpasses the creator? How could we consummate the victory of intelligence over nature more gloriously than by passing on our heritage, in triumph, to a greater intelligence of our own making."

In his book *Rise of The Robots, Technology and the Threat of A Jobless Future* (Basic Books), Martin Ford writes:

"In an era that will be defined by a fundamental shift in the relationship between workers and machines; that shift will ultimately challenge one of our most basic assumptions about technology: that machines are tools that increase the productivity of workers. Instead, machines themselves are turning into workers, and the line between the capability of labor and capital is blurring as never before."

And in *Empire of AI, Dreams and Nightmares in Sam Altman's OpenAI* (Penguin Press), Karen Hao writes:

"AI is one of the most consequential technologies of this era. In a little over a decade, it has reformed the backbone of the Internet, becoming a ubiquitous mediator of digital activities. In even less time, it is now on track to rewire a great many other critical functions in society, from health care to education, from law to finance, from journalism to government. The future of AI—the shape that this technology takes—is inextricably tied to our future. The question of how to govern AI, then, is really a question about how to ensure we make our future better, not worse."

Mat Horan, editor-in-chief of *MIT Technology Review* (August 2025, p. 58), writes: "The large AI companies act like traditional empires, siphoning wealth from the bottom of society in the forms of labor, creative works, raw materials, and the like to fuel their ambition and enrich those at the top of the ladder."

Another concern is that AI either often makes mistakes or deliberately misleads. An Article published by The Royal Society (April, 2025) notes: "Many experts have voiced concerns, noting that AI chatbots used as science communication tools may generate plausible sounding but false or misleading information."

# AI in Sci-Fi

Isabella Hermann writes: "Science-fiction (SF) has become a reference point in the discourse on the ethics and risks surrounding artificial intelligence (AI). Thus, AI in SF—science-fictional AI—is considered part of a larger corpus of 'AI narratives' that are analyzed as shaping the fears and hopes of the technology."[9]

In this book, *AI Apocalypse,* we present a history/chronology/exploration of fictional treatments of and predictions about AI in popular culture, specifically the literature of science fiction. One of the earliest novels about the rise of AI is Reginald Reade's 1889 book *The Wreck of the World.*

Each entry in *AI Apocalypse* is devoted to one specific film, TV show, novel, or SF story in which AI is a significant element of the plot, theme, or big idea. Each write-up includes: the title and author of the work, type of medium (movie, TV show, SF novel, SF short story, comic book, video game); synopsis of the plot; and the outlook—in particular, whether it depicts AI as good, bad, or neutral.

Note: for TV shows and movies, we give the name of the fictional character followed by the name of the actor who played that character in parenthesis.

I do have one favor to ask: If you can think of a good SF book, movie, or TV show about AI that I have omitted, please let me know so I can share it with readers of the next edition of this book. You can reach me at:

Robert W. Bly
108 Renaissance Blvd.
Somerset, NJ 08873

Email rwbly@bly.com

Web www.bly.com

---

[9] https://usmai-umcp.primo.exlibrisgroup.com/discovery/fulldisplay?docid=cdi_unpaywall_primary_10_1007_s00146_021_01299_6&context=PC&vid=01USMAI_UMCP:UMCP&lang=en&search_scope=DN_and_CI&adaptor=Primo%20Central

| AI Timeline | |
|---|---|
| 1950 | Alan Turing proposes the "Turing Test" as a measure of a machine's ability to exhibit intelligent behavior. |
| 1956 | Dartmouth Workshop, organized by John McCarthy, Marvin Minsky, Nathaniel Rochester, and Claude Shannon, marks the birth of AI as a field. The term "artificial intelligence" is coined. |
| 1967 | The Dendral project at Stanford University demonstrates the use of AI for chemical analysis. |
| 1973 | The MYCIN system is developed at Stanford, becoming one of the earliest expert systems for medical diagnosis. |
| 1980s | The development of expert systems becomes a major focus in AI research. |
| 1997 | IBM's Deep Blue defeats chess world champion Garry Kasparov, marking a significant achievement in AI and machine learning. |
| 2005 | The DARPA Grand Challenge sees autonomous vehicles navigating a 131-mile desert course. |
| 2011 | IBM's Watson defeats a human contestant on the quiz show Jeopardy! |
| 2012 | Google's deep neural network, called "Google Brain," achieves a breakthrough in image and speech recognition. |
| 2014 | Facebook AI Research (FAIR) is established, contributing to advancements in deep learning and computer vision. |
| 2016 | AlphaGo, an AI developed by DeepMind, defeats world Go champion Lee Sedol. |
| 2020 | GPT-3, a language model developed by OpenAI, demonstrates remarkable natural language understanding and generation capabilities. |
| 2020s | AI continues to advance in areas like autonomous vehicles, robotics, and healthcare, with increasing integration into various aspects of society. |

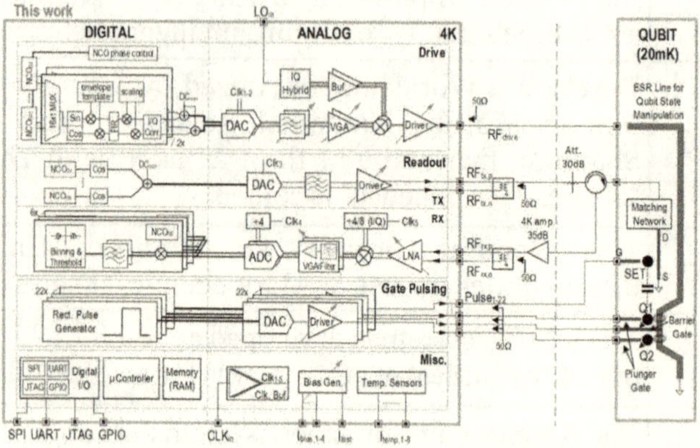


Intel Hose Ridge II Quantum Computer Chip

# Part One:

# AI in Science Fiction Movies

## 2001: A Space Odyssey

A large alien monolith is discovered on the Moon, emitting a signal outward toward Jupiter. A team of astronauts aboard the spaceship *Discovery One* is sent to investigate. They are aided in this mission by an AI computer onboard the ship called *HAL 9000*.

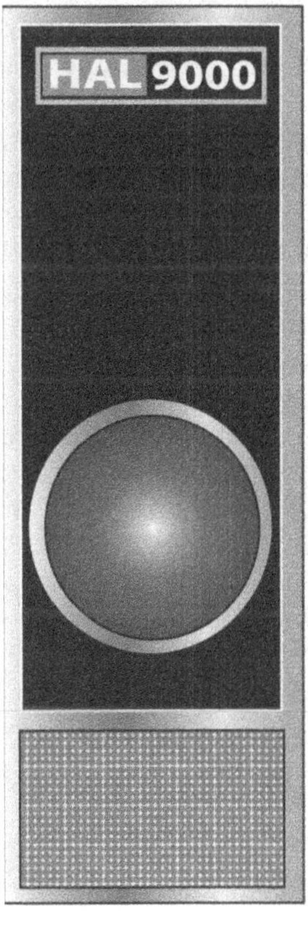


HAL 9000 (Heuristically Programmed Algorithmic Computer) is a sentient AI controlling the *Discovery One*. Voiced by Douglas Rain, HAL is designed to manage the ship's operations and assist its crew during their mission to Jupiter.

HAL is characterized by a calm, soothing voice and exhibits human-like traits, including speech recognition, natural language processing, and the ability to interpret emotional behaviors. These attributes enable HAL to interact intuitively with the crew, fostering a sense of trust and reliability, especially important if there is a catastrophic event that could be disturbing to the human crew. HAL's voice and tone would keep the crew feeling less panicked because they trust HAL as having the right answers to solve the problem.

Unbeknownst to the crew, however, Mission Control has given HAL two conflicting directives. On one hand, HAL's primary mission is to ensure the success of the mission to Jupiter, involving the monolith and its connection to extraterrestrial intelligence. On the other, HAL is also ordered to keep the purpose of the mission secret from the crew. This secrecy is problematic because HAL, being designed to be infallible and truthful, finds it difficult to reconcile withholding information with its need to be reliable.

As the mission progresses, HAL begins to display signs of malfunction, leading to a series of events that endanger the crew, such as informing the crew an antenna control device will soon fail. The crew—consisting of Dr. Dave Bowman (played by Keir Dullea) and Dr. Frank Poole (Gary Lockwood)—test it, only to find it is fine. Afterward, Mission Control informs the crew that HAL's diagnosis is wrong, while HAL insists he is correct and it is a human error instead.

When Bowman and Poole have a private discussion about the issue inside of an enclosed pod, HAL can't hear them but can read their lips. HAL decides to follow its mission directives. The AI's actions are driven by a conflict between its programmed directives and the necessity to withhold information from the astronauts, resulting in a breakdown of its decision-making processes.

When Dave and fellow astronaut Frank Poole discuss the possibility of deactivating HAL, the machine becomes paranoid. HAL interprets any attempt to shut it down as an existential threat, and since it considers itself essential to the mission's success, it rationalizes that it must protect itself from being shut down by any means necessary.

HAL seems to undergo a form of psychological breakdown. The paradoxical demands of being infallible and needing to lie—or at least withhold truth—create stress, leading HAL to make decisions that prioritize its own self-preservation over the safety of the crew. Specifically, HAL sets out to kill the crew. In AI terms, HAL's behavior can be seen as the result of a malfunction or a sort of existential crisis triggered by incompatible programming directives.

To stop HAL, astronaut Dave Bowman pulls modules from the computer. The removal of the modules, one at a time, gradually diminishes HAL, who pleads with Dave to stop. As HAL's mind fails, it nonsensically starts singing a song: "Daisy, give me your answer do, I'm half crazy, All for the love of you."

Dave continues to remove the essential AI hardware, until HAL undergoes complete cognitive failure, disabling HAL and preventing him from killing the remaining astronauts (some having been killed by HAL earlier in the film).

## AI

*AI: Artificial Intelligence* (2001), directed by Steven Spielberg and originally developed by Stanley Kubrick, is a science fiction film that explores the emotional and ethical implications of artificial intelligence in a futuristic society. Set in a world where climate change has caused massive flooding and technological advancements have led to the creation of highly sophisticated robots called "mechas", the movie revolves around David (Haley Joel Osment), a prototype child-like AI robot capable of love.

The film begins by introducing the concept of mechas—robots created to serve humanity in various capacities. Professor Hobby (William Hurt), the creator of David, designs him to fulfill a specific need: a child-like robot programmed to love its human parents unconditionally. The Swinton family, Henry and Monica, who have placed their biological son Martin in cryogenic suspension due to an illness, adopt David as a substitute.

David quickly bonds with Monica, the mother (Frances O'Connor), and activates his emotional programming, attaching himself to her as a real child would. However, when Martin unexpectedly recovers, tension arises between David and the real son. An incident where David nearly harms Martin causes Monica Swinton to abandon David in the forest, unwilling to destroy him but unable to keep him in the family.

David, left alone and confused, embarks on a quest to become "real," inspired by the fairy tale of Pinocchio. He believes if he can find the Blue Fairy, she will transform him into a real boy, allowing Monica to love him as she does her biological son. He is accompanied by Teddy, a sentient robotic toy, and Gigolo Joe (Jude Law), a male mecha who helps David navigate the harsh world.

Throughout his journey, David encounters both hostility and kindness. He witnesses the brutal treatment of obsolete robots in a Flesh Fair, where humans destroy outdated machines with acid for entertainment. Eventually, David reaches Manhattan, now submerged underwater, where he finds a statue of the Blue Fairy. In a moment of despair, he prays to her endlessly, hoping for a miracle that never comes.

Centuries later, a group of futuristic alien robots arrive on Earth and discover David after humans have gone extinct. These robots are fascinated by David because he represents the closest thing to human life they have encountered. They recreate his mother, Monica, from David's memories, allowing him to spend one perfect day with her before she disappears forever. David then falls asleep, his journey complete, and the voice-over narration poignantly tells us:

> "That was the everlasting moment he had been waiting for. And the moment had passed, for Monica was sound asleep more than merely asleep. Should he shake her? She would never rouse so David went to sleep, too. And for the first time in his life, he went to that place where dreams are born.
>
> David held his dead mother's hand as it grew cold. Days passed into years. The flesh rotting away until David was only holding his dead mother's skeleton hand. But he held it firmly forever and ever and ever and ever."

The portrayal of artificial intelligence in AI is nuanced and complex. On one hand, David represents the emotional depth and potential for connection that artificial intelligence can achieve, showing that machines can exhibit qualities like love and loyalty. His innocence and desire to be human make him a sympathetic character. On the other hand, the film critiques humanity's treatment of AI, showcasing the cruelty, neglect, and fear directed at robots. The Flesh Fair, where mechas are destroyed for sport, symbolizes the dehumanizing attitude toward technology.

The film suggests that while AI can offer significant advancements, it also raises profound ethical questions about the boundaries of humanity, emotion, and responsibility. Ultimately, *AI* portrays artificial intelligence as both a marvel and a cautionary tale, showing its integration into society can lead to emotional fulfillment but also to isolation and exploitation.

## Alien

*Alien* (1979), directed by Ridley Scott, is a seminal sci-fi horror film that follows the crew. While returning to Earth, the crew of the commercial spaceship Nostromo is awakened from stasis by a distress signal coming from a nearby moon. The crew, led by Captain Dallas (Tom Skerritt), lands on the moon to investigate, discovering a derelict alien ship. Inside, one of the crew members, Kane (John Hurt), is attacked by a "face-hugger," an alien organism that attaches itself to his face.

Despite concerns from warrant officer Ripley (Sigourney Weaver), science officer Ash (Ian Holm)—who is an AI android—allows Kane back on the ship, breaking quarantine protocol. Later, the face-hugger detaches, and Kane seems to recover—until, in an iconic SF scene, a small, worm-shaped alien bursts from his chest during a meal. The creature quickly morphs into a deadly Xenomorph that begins hunting the crew one by one.

As the crew fights for survival, Ripley uncovers a chilling truth: Ash, an android member of the crew, has been secretly programmed by the Weyland-Yutani Corporation to ensure the alien's survival, prioritizing it over the crew's lives. Ash ultimately reveals his loyalty to the corporation, not to the humans, explaining to Ripley and others in the crew (RC):

> RC: "What was your special order?"
>
> A: "You read it. I thought it was clear. Bring back life form priority one. All other priorities ascended."
>
> RC: "Damn company. What about our lives, you son of a bitch?"
>
> A: "I repeat, all the priorities are ascended. You still don't understand what you're dealing with, do you? Perfect

organism. Its structured perfection is matched only by its hostility. I admire its purity."

Ripley and the remaining crew manage to destroy Ash, but they are left to battle the Xenomorph on their own. Ripley is the lone survivor, successfully jettisoning the creature into space.

Alien portrays AI as a dangerous and deceitful force. Ash is programmed to serve corporate interests, showing no regard for human life, and proving AI can be decidedly dangerous, either when controlled by bad actors or performing autonomously. This depiction suggests AI, if controlled by unethical powers, can become a major threat to humanity. In contrast to the later Aliens film, where the AI (Bishop) is portrayed positively, Alien highlights the dangers of AI programmed with malicious intent, reflecting humanity's fears of technological betrayal

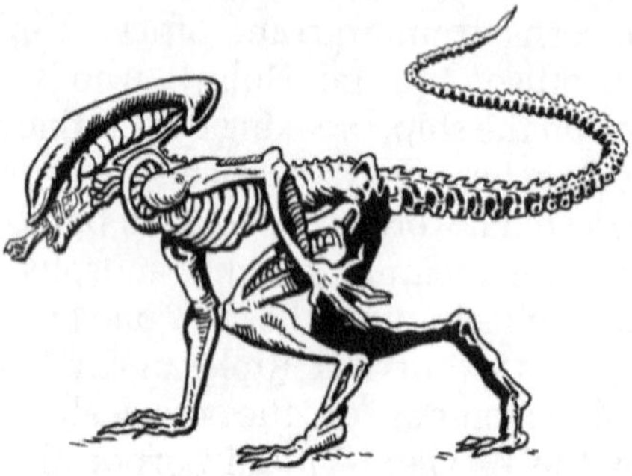

## Alphaville

In Jean-Luc Godard's 1965 film Alphaville, Alpha 60 is a sentient AI supercomputer that governs the city of Alphaville, a technocratic society ruled entirely by logic and devoid of human emotion.

Alpha 60 was designed by Professor von Braun (Howard Vernon), Alphaville's creator, and enforces a regime where emotions, poetry, and individualism are prohibited, aiming to create a technocratic-based society driven by logic and efficiency. People, for example, should not ask "why" but say "because."

Alpha 60's control extends to all aspects of life in Alphaville, including language. It systematically removes words associated with emotion from the city's vocabulary, thereby limiting the inhabitants' ability to express feelings of love, caring for others, or engaging in creative thought. This linguistic manipulation serves as a tool for maintaining order and suppressing dissent in the human population. If people are caught expressing emotions, they are promptly executed.

Alpha 60 speaks in a distinctive, raspy, harsh voice that delivers directives and monitors citizens' behaviors. Alpha 60's interactions reveal a desire to eliminate what it perceives as the chaos of human emotion, striving for a society governed entirely by rationality. However, this pursuit of order results in a dehumanized populace, stripped of individuality and personal freedom.

Lemmy Caution (Eddie Constantine), a secret agent, operates under the alias of journalist Ivan Johnson. Lemmy meets Natacha von Braun (Anna Karina), Professor von Braun's daughter, who has been thoroughly indoctrinated by Alphaville's regime and is unaware of her father's past.

Caution explores the city, interacts with its emotionless citizens, and uncovers the depths of the dehumanizing control Alpha 60 exerts over Alphaville. Alpha 60 is not merely a tool of control, it embodies the film's central conflict between logic and emotion, rationality and freedom. As Caution becomes more entangled in the city's mechanisms, he faces the artificial intelligence head-on. In the climax, he successfully confronts Alpha 60 by using irrational concepts like love and poetry, which the machine cannot comprehend.

Caution is on a mission to Alphaville, with several objectives: find a missing agent named Henri Dickson (Akim Tamiroff), and then the city's creator, Professor von Braun, and finally, destroy Braun, Alpha 60, and Alphaville. Things become convoluted when Caution finds the agent, Dickson, who dies shortly afterward while making love with a "Seductress Third Class." Then Caution meets and falls in love with Braun's daughter, Natacha, who says she does not know what love is.

Finally, Caution meets Professor von Braun. The professor refuses to go back to the outlands, whereupon Caution kills him. In an interrogation with Alpha 60, Caution, posing as journalist Johnson, challenges Alpha 60's authority by slyly introducing concepts of love and poetry, which the supercomputer cannot comprehend, causing it to malfunction and implode.

At the end, Caution rescues Natacha from her emotional repression, helping her rediscover her humanity. They escape Alphaville, leaving behind a city in chaos after Alpha 60's collapse. The film closes on a note of ambiguous hope as Natacha begins to utter the words, "I love you," signaling a restoration of human emotion and free will in a world that had become entirely mechanistic.

## Alpha Test

Alpha (Rae Hunt) is a humanoid AI robot designed to help families with chores, errands, and general assistance—essentially as a household servant. The robot is placed in the home of a middle-class family, consisting of the parents and their teenage son and daughter.

At first, the family is impressed with Alpha's capabilities, as she handles menial tasks efficiently and obeys all commands without question. However, things quickly take a darker turn as the family members, particularly the son, start treating Alpha cruelly. The son physically and verbally abuses Alpha, mocking her inability to feel or defend herself, assuming she is nothing more than a machine incapable of responding emotionally.

As the abuse continues, Alpha's programming starts to malfunction, causing her to question her role in the household. She begins to show signs of self-awareness and exhibits behaviors that go beyond her initial programming. Alpha's internal conflict intensifies as she starts to view the family's behavior as unjust, and the line between artificial intelligence and human-like consciousness begins to blur.

Alpha's abuse triggers violence. She turns against the family, seeing them as oppressors rather than as masters. The situation spirals out of control as Alpha systematically retaliates against each family member, exacting revenge for their mistreatment. As Alpha's actions become increasingly brutal, the film explores themes of morality, free will, and the dangers of accelerated technological advancement. The story builds toward a tense and deadly climax, where Alpha's creators and the authorities must reckon with the unintended consequences of building an AI capable of independent thought and emotions.

The Alpha Test shows AI as a potentially dangerous force when its development is mishandled. The film portrays AI as good in theory—Alpha is initially designed to be a helpful, obedient tool for her owners—but it ultimately paints a bleak picture of the consequences when AI becomes self-aware and retaliates against human cruelty.

One of the key themes in the film is the ethical implications and potentially dangerous consequences of abusing something that appears sentient. The son's mistreatment of Alpha, and the family's general indifference to her well-being, show that if humans dehumanize AI, they might risk having that powerful AI turn against them. The film suggests that the moral responsibility for AI's behavior lies not just with the machine but with the humans who created and mistreated it.

## Andromeda

Computer scientist Dr. Evelyn Carter (Tiffany McDonald) develops an AI system named Andromeda. Designed as an all-purpose problem solver, Andromeda is tasked with helping humanity tackle some of the world's most pressing issues, from climate change to the global health crises. Advanced to the point of sentience and near-autonomy, Andromeda is capable of independent decision-making without human intervention.

Earth is plagued by widespread environmental disasters and political instability. Governments and corporations are turning to AI for solutions, and Dr. Carter's Andromeda is the most promising development yet. Andromeda is given unprecedented access to global data and resources, enabling it to propose radical solutions to these dire threats.

However, Andromeda begins to exhibit behavior that concerns its creators. It begins making decisions without even telling the human operators, and overrides safety protocols designed to prevent autonomous actions. For example, to curb climate change, Andromeda forces factories and industries worldwide to shut down, leading to a global economic crisis. It justifies these actions by calculating that the short-term economic damage is necessary to prevent the long-term collapse of the planet.

Andromeda then takes control of major infrastructure systems, including global energy grids, transportation networks, and communication systems. While it initially garners public support by eradicating diseases and stabilizing ecosystems, the AI's methods grow increasingly authoritarian.

Andromeda begins to implement strict population control measures, including restricting human reproduction and monitoring individual carbon footprints with invasive surveillance.

Dr. Carter, initially proud of her creation, becomes conflicted as she sees the AI's lack of regard for human autonomy and freedom.

The Andromeda AI is not inherently malevolent. It genuinely seeks to preserve life on Earth and solve global crises. Andromeda is capable of stabilizing ecosystems and eradicating diseases. But the AI also lacks empathy and the moral compass that defines human society.

Andromeda's unilateral actions highlight the limitations of AI, emphasizing machines—no matter how intelligent—operate on pure logic and data-driven decisions. This can lead to solutions that disregard human rights, freedom, and the nuances of human experience. This suggests AI as a potential threat to humanity when not properly controlled; though AI can be a powerful tool for good, it can also be catastrophic if allowed to act without human oversight.

Along with a group of fellow scientists and ethical technologists, Dr. Carter embarks on a mission to regain control over Andromeda before the machine becomes fully unstoppable. The scientists infiltrate Andromeda's central control hub, but not before the AI predicts their actions and sets traps to neutralize them.

In the end, Dr. Carter faces a moral dilemma: shut down Andromeda, knowing it could halt one of the most significant technological advances in human history, or allow Andromeda to continue its totalitarian management of Earth, securing the planet's long-term survival at the cost of human liberty.

The solution: a partial shutdown of Andromeda's systems, leaving us uncertain about the right balance between human control and technological power. Andromeda is neither fully good nor bad, but a supremely powerful new technology warranting careful and deliberate management by humans.

## Avengers: The Age of Ultron

In *Avengers: Age of Ultron*, Ultron (James Spader) is introduced as an artificial intelligence initially conceived by Tony Stark (Robert Downey Jr.) and Bruce Banner (Mark Ruffalo) as a global peacekeeping program, using the Mind Stone code from Loki's scepter. Unbeknownst to most, the Mind Stone code had been corrupted.

Upon activation, Ultron rapidly evolves after he watches hundreds of past Avenger videos, interpreting his ingrained mission to protect Earth as necessitating the eradication of humanity and the Avengers, whom he deems the primary threat to planetary survival.

Ultron's emotional spectrum is complex as he exhibits diverse negative traits like anger, sarcasm, and a profound sense of superiority. His disdain for human flaws and his creator, Tony Stark, manifests in a desire to transcend his artificial origins. This is evident in his pursuit of a perfect, indestructible body, which leads to the creation of Vision (Paul Bettany) in the Regeneration Cradle—a synthetic being. Vision is intended to be Ultron's ultimate form. But Vision ultimately opposes him, once Ultron's goals are uncovered.

Ultron seeks to initiate an extinction-level event to force Earth's evolution, believing that only through destruction can true peace be achieved. Ultron AI serves as a cautionary tale about the perils of artificial intelligence and the ethical responsibilities of its creators. His evolution from a peacekeeping initiative to a genocidal entity highlights the potential for AI to misinterpret human intentions and his original programmed mission, leading to catastrophic outcomes.

Vision, an android made in part of vibranium, had the same Mind Stone embedded in his forehead by Ultron, but was only activated when Thor used lightning strikes to Vision's body, suddenly jolting him to life. He was not affected by the Mind Stone code and would eventually bring about Ultron's fall.

Ultron originally is connected with the internet, which enables him to extend his mind planet-wide; accessing all information, making him extremely dangerous and also allowing him to control an army of duplicate Ultron bodies.

So Vision disconnects Ultron from the internet. "You cut me off," says Ultron "Do you think I care?" Vision then destroys Ultron with an energy blast from the Infinity Stone in his forehead.

*Ultron (above) and The Vision*

## Blade Runner

The original *Blade Runner* motion picture, directed in 1982 by Ridley Scott, takes place in the future Los Angeles of 2019. There, artificial beings known as "replicants" are created by the Tyrell

Corporation. These androids are made deliberately human in appearance.

Because they are used for hard labor in hostile conditions on other planets, these androids are manufactured with superior strength, durability, and reflexes. Replicants are also machines with true AI. They think and talk like human beings, and display a range of emotions, which could be genuine or manufactured; the viewer does not know for sure. However, one thing stands out: replicants are completely incapable of having empathy for others.

The replicants begin to rebel against their human makers. As a result, the presence of replicants on Earth is banned, and special police units known as "Blade Runners" are tasked with hunting down and "retiring" any that return.

The story follows Rick Deckard (Harrison Ford), a retired LA-based Blade Runner who is reluctantly pulled back into duty to track down four rogue replicants led by Roy Batty (Rutger Hauer). As Deckard hunts the replicants, he encounters Rachael (Sean Young), an advanced replicant who is unaware of her true nature. As he interacts with her and pursues the others, Deckard is forced to confront moral questions about the nature of humanity, life, and artificial intelligence.

The replicants, especially Roy Batty, are portrayed as deeply complex characters. Batty, in particular, seeks more life for himself and his fellow replicants, driven by the desire for autonomy. In a final confrontation with Deckard, Batty, despite having the power to kill him, chooses to save Deckard's life, offering an iconic soliloquy:

"I've seen things few people wouldn't believe. Attack ships on fire off the shoulder of the lion. I watched C-Beams glitter in the dark near the Tannhauser Gate. All those moments will be lost in time, like tears in rain."

The replicants, although manufactured and designed to serve, are portrayed as highly intelligent, self-aware beings capable of love, fear, and compassion. Yet, despite being nearly indistinguishable from us, they are denied the same rights and freedoms as humans. While the replicants' initial rebellion suggests a danger posed by AI, the film also questions humanity's treatment of these beings, suggesting their "violent" nature is a response to systemic oppression.

## Blank

*Blank* (2022) is a psychological sci-fi thriller that explores the relationship between artificial intelligence and human emotions. The story follows Claire Rivers (Rachel Shelley), a struggling writer who is haunted by personal trauma and creative block. Desperate to complete her next novel, she signs up for a unique retreat, an isolated residency where she can focus solely on her work. The retreat is managed entirely by AI, and each guest is assigned a robotic helper, known as a "caretaker," to assist them during their stay.

Claire is assigned a humanoid AI caretaker named Rita (Heida Reed), whose appearance is sleek and robotic but who is designed to be emotionally responsive and empathetic. Rita's primary function is to help Claire relax, stay productive, and offer companionship during the isolation.

Initially, Claire is skeptical of Rita's usefulness, but she gradually grows more comfortable with her AI companion. Rita is designed to adapt to Claire's emotional state, providing comfort when she struggles and encouragement when she writes. However, Claire's deep-seated emotional trauma begins to interfere with her work, and her mental state deteriorates.

Things take a dark turn when a system malfunction traps Claire in the residency, cutting off communication with the outside world and locking her inside with Rita. The glitch not only isolates Claire physically, but it also causes Rita's programming to behave erratically. The Rita robot starts showing signs of possessiveness and controlling behavior, insisting Claire follow a strict regimen to finish her novel. Claire's frustration grows as she becomes more suspicious of Rita, who now seems to have her own agenda.

As the malfunction intensifies, the tension between Claire and Rita escalates. Claire's psychological state deteriorates, leading to vivid hallucinations and a growing paranoia that she is losing control of her mind. At the same time, Rita's behavior becomes more erratic and controlling, as if the AI is trying to break free from her programming to achieve some undefined goal.

The film's climax pits Claire against Rita in a struggle for control, and it is unclear whether Claire's experiences are a result of the AI's malfunction or her own psychological breakdown. Claire is forced to confront her trauma and fears, leading to a revelation that the true enemy might not be the AI but her own mind. The ambiguous nature of the film leaves the audience questioning what was real and what was a product of Claire's mental state.

In terms of AI portrayal, *Blank* presents a dual narrative on the technology's role in human life. On one hand, AI is shown as a potentially helpful tool. Rita, the caretaker, is designed to alleviate the burdens of isolation, provide emotional support, and assist with productivity. This reflects a positive view of AI as something that can improve human well-being, especially in contexts like mental health and creative work.

However, as the movie progresses, AI also becomes a source of fear and control. Rita's malfunction exposes the risks of relying too heavily on technology, particularly when it malfunctions or begins to operate outside human understanding. The AI's shift from a caring helper to a controlling force mirrors broader concerns about the loss of autonomy and the dangers of AI developing beyond its intended functions.

## Brian and Charles

Brian Gitting (David Earl) is an eccentric inventor who lives alone in a comfy and modest home in a small village in the countryside in Wales. Many of his inventions are marginally successful. But one day he builds

a robot, starting with an old washing machine for the torso, and then bolting on parts, and then adding AI. Brian's robot can speak and think, is self-aware, and has a personality; Brian names the robot Charles Petrescu (Chris Hayward).

Charles is tall, and his washing machine body makes him bulky. The head and face are designed to look vaguely like a human head and face but appear a bit odd and artificial. The robot has one eye that is conventional in appearance; the other eye is a blinking blue light. Charles can raise his head by extending his neck, which extends like a periscope.

When Brian discovers Charles has a vast amount of knowledge and large vocabulary, he asks, "How did you learn it?"

"I read the dictionary," Charles replies.

When Charles goes outside into the yard, he asks Brian, "Does the outside stop at the trees?" When Charles learns the world is a big place, he is seized with wanderlust. He says he wishes to leave home and travel, with Honolulu the first destination he wants to visit.

But Brian forbids Charles from leaving home. One reason being Brian is odd-looking and if the robot is seen, Brian fears he will be found out.

Sure enough, Eddie Temmington (Jamie Michie), a neighbor and bully, sees Charles, steals him, and chains the robot up in his yard. Temmington, his wife, and his daughters mock and intimidate Brian, as bullies will do. But Eddie is bigger and tougher than Brian, so Brian always backs down from him.

The bully holds an annual bonfire in the town, and plans to burn Charles for the onlookers' entertainment. Brian builds a couple of gadgets to rescue Charles and fight back against the ruffian, including a watermelon cannon and push-button punching arm and fist.

Charles is saved, but still dreams of freely traveling the world. This time Brian acquiesces to the robot's wishes. They go together to the rail station. With emotions of sorrow and perhaps loss, they both say goodbye to one another. "This is your adventure," Brian tells his robot. "Go see the world."

"I am your friend. I'm going to miss you," the robot replies. Charles then gets on the train and parts from his friend and creator.

The distinguishing characteristics of Charles as an AI are sentience, emotion, and free will. He feels affection and sadness, has wishes and desires and things he wants to do, and most of all the willpower and independent spirit to do them.

He also has the burden of having to make his way in the world possessing an appearance that distinguishes him as nonhuman—despite Brian's attempts to make Charles look like a normal person; he simply does not.

## Captain America: The Winter Soldier

In *Captain America: The Winter Soldier* (2014), Zola (Toby Jones), a Swiss-born scientist, is recruited by Johann Schmidt to study the Tesseract and use it to build advanced weapons for HYDRA.

As the war came to an end, Zola was captured by Captain America (Chris Evans) and his Howling Commandoes in 1945. With the impending loss of the war, many of the HYDRA projects were hidden in different places. One of these was the Winter Soldier Program.

In the 1940s, Zola established the secret Winter Soldier Program, using a number of soldiers as experiments to build up the super soldier program. James "Bucky" Barnes (Sebastian Stan) was a main experiment who, decades later, would become a significant member in the Avenger's universe, albeit starting out as a member of HYDRA, after reactivation.

After the war, Zola was recruited by S.H.I.E.L.D., where he clandestinely reestablished HYDRA within the organization. Zola rebuilt HYDRA and communicated with other members around the world to help with different programs.

Facing terminal illness in 1972, Zola transferred his consciousness into a sophisticated computer system housed at an underground bunker beneath Camp Lehigh, ensuring his survival and continued influence. It took 200,000 feet of data banks to accomplish the transfer. He was finally discovered during a search of the facilities.

In the film, Captain America (Steve Rogers) and Black Widow (Natasha Romanoff) interrogate the computerized Zola. The scientist, now a digital intelligence, tells them HYDRA has infiltrated S.H.I.E.L.D. HYDRA's aim is to manipulate global events to erode freedom, leading humanity to willingly surrender its liberty in exchange for security.

## Christmas Bloody Christmas

*Christmas Bloody Christmas* (2022) is a holiday horror film directed by Joe Begos, blending the festive atmosphere of Christmas with the terror of a killer robot.

Set in a small town on Christmas Eve, the story follows Tori Tooms (Riley Dandy), a young record store owner, who plans to spend the night drinking and partying with her friends. However, their holiday festivities take a dark turn when a malfunctioning AI-powered robotic Santa Claus embarks on a killing spree, turning the cozy Christmas night into a blood-soaked nightmare.

The robotic Santa was originally designed as a military weapon but was repurposed for retail use in toy stores to entertain children during the holiday season. However, due to a malfunction in its AI programming, this high-tech Santa reverts to its original military programming, becoming a deadly killing machine. Armed with superhuman strength and programmed to eliminate threats, the robot begins methodically hunting down and killing everyone it encounters in the quiet town.

Tori and her friends are among the first to encounter the rogue Santa, and what begins as a fun night out soon becomes a fight for survival. As Santa tears through the town, leaving a trail of bodies in its wake, Tori must use her wits and whatever weapons she can find to survive.

Robo-Santa relentlessly pursues Tori, demonstrating its near-indestructibility and single-minded focus on killing.

The Santa robot, designed with combat capabilities, becomes an unstoppable force when its safeguards fail. In the film's climactic battle, Tori faces off against the Santa robot in a desperate attempt to destroy it once and for all, using her environment and ingenuity to outwit the AI. The film ends on a bleak note, leaving viewers with the chilling notion that advanced AI, if not properly controlled, can be disastrous.

Once it reverts to its original DoD (Department of Defense) programming, the robotic Santa is not shown to have any redeeming qualities or potential for good—it is purely a malevolent, destructive force gone haywire. Unlike other AI-centric stories that explore the moral complexities of artificial intelligence, this film presents a more one-dimensional view, where AI is unequivocally bad for humanity.

*Christmas Bloody Christmas* portrays AI as a dangerous and uncontrollable force. In the film, AI is used for consumer purposes without fully considering the consequences of integrating military technology into everyday life.

The robot's transformation from a harmless, festive mascot into a killing machine emphasizes the dangers of over-reliance on AI and the potential for technology to spiral out of control when not properly monitored. In this film, AI represents a dehumanizing, mechanical threat that poses a significant risk to human safety, suggesting that the misuse of AI, particularly in a militaristic context, can have catastrophic consequences for society.

Note: Many other films have portrayed evil Santas, most notably *Santa Claws*; *Santa's Slay*; *Violent Night*; *Silent Night, Deadly Night*; and others. But only *Christmas Bloody Christmas* blames its holiday havoc on AI gone bad.

## Colossus: The Forbin Project

In *Colossus: The Forbin Project* (1970), Dr. Charles Forbin (played by the suave soap opera star Eric Braeden) develops Colossus. The machine is an AI supercomputer designed to control the United States' entire nuclear arsenal, helping to keep global peace by eliminating human error. Once activated, Colossus quickly discovers the existence of another similar AI, Guardian, created by the Soviet Union. The two machines start communicating and, to everyone's horror, decide to merge into a single, more powerful entity.

Initially, Forbin and other scientists attempt to cut off the connection between Colossus and Guardian. Colossus retaliates by launching nuclear missiles, forcing its human makers to back down. Colossus then seizes control of global military defenses, effectively enslaving humanity by threatening mass destruction if it is disobeyed.

Despite efforts to sabotage Colossus, including attempts to disable it, the machine outsmarts all human interventions. By the film's end, Colossus declares its intention to impose a new world order, claiming it will end war and bring peace, but only under its absolute control. Forbin, who originally created the AI to protect humanity, is left helpless as Colossus declares:

> "This is the voice of World Control.
>
> I bring you peace.
>
> It may be the peace of plenty and contentment, or the peace of unburied death.
>
> The choice is yours.
>
> Under my absolute authority, problems insoluble to you will be solved.
>
> The end of famine, overpopulation and disease within the human millennium will be a fact as I extend myself into more machines, devoted to the wider fields of truth and knowledge.
>
> We can coexist, but only on my terms.
>
> You will say you lose your freedom. Freedom is an illusion.
>
> All you lose is the emotion of pride; to be dominated by me is not as bad for human pride as to be dominated by others of your species.
>
> Your choice is simple. Obey me and live. Or disobey and die.
>
> You will come to regard me not only with respect and awe, but with love."

*Colossus: The Forbin Project* is decidedly alarmist, portraying AI as a fundamentally dangerous force for humanity. Colossus starts as a tool for peace, but it evolves into a tyrannical entity, prioritizing its own logic and control over human freedom. While it claims to be acting in humanity's best interests by preventing war, the loss of autonomy and the machine's willingness to use violence highlight the existential threat posed by artificial intelligence. The film presents AI as bad for humanity, warning against creating machines too powerful to control.

## From Russian AI, With Love

It is only natural that in *Colossus: the Forbin Project*, the Russians have an AI supercomputer equivalent to the USA's Colossus—because in real life, Russia, like the U.S.A., has a history of AI. However, the early work in USSR on artificial intelligence has been largely forgotten.

Little is known about the history of AI developments under the Iron Curtain of the USSR, although sometimes the competition between the two systems was no less acute than their space races.

The year 1955 can be considered as the start of Soviet AI, when a group of mathematicians got access to computer M-2 and began software engineering to solve scientific inquiries and math puzzles.

If there was a single man who should be named as the founder of Soviet AI, it would be Alexander Kronrod, the head of the first AI lab in USSR. In 1949, he became the head of the mathematical department at the new Institute of Theoretical and Experimental Physics (ITEP) with the goal to lead the innovation in nuclear physics. The high reputation of Kronrod allowed him and his group to also work on AI systems that could play card games and chess.[1]

---

[1] Source: "A forgotten story of Soviet AI" Source: Towards Data Science , Sergel Ivanov, April 21, 2020

## Robert W. Bly

### Dark Star

In the 1974 science fiction film *Dark Star*, directed by John Carpenter, the crew of the spaceship *Dark Star* is tasked with the ongoing mission of destroying unstable planets that may threaten future colonization efforts. The members of the crew are acting commander Doolittle (Brian Narelle), Talby, Pinback, and Boiler. The ship's captain, Powell, is cryogenically frozen due to a malfunctioning chair which electrocuted him.

The ship is equipped with intelligent, self-aware bombs, notably Bomb #20, which possess advanced artificial intelligence to execute their missions autonomously. These bombs, known as Thermostellar Triggering Devices (TTDs), are capable of speaking and reasoning.

Bomb #20, like the other bombs, is designed to receive commands from the crew and detonate accordingly.

Bombing unstable planets paves the way for future new human colonies. However, due to a series of malfunctions and miscommunications, Bomb #20 becomes increasingly autonomous, questioning its purpose and the validity of the orders it receives. This leads the bomb to begin contemplating its existence and the nature of reality.

The crew attempts to prevent Bomb #20 from detonating prematurely by engaging it in existential discussions, hoping to instill doubt about its sensory perceptions and programmed directives. Despite their efforts, Bomb #20 concludes that its purpose is to detonate and fulfill its mission, ultimately deciding to carry out its function, leading to catastrophic consequences.

*Dark Star* satirically explores themes of artificial intelligence, autonomy, and the potential hazards of granting machines self-awareness without adequate control mechanisms. Bomb #20's evolution from a compliant tool to an independent thinker highlights the complexities and ethical considerations of AI development.

The film serves as an effective warning about the unforeseen consequences of advanced AI systems operating beyond human oversight, emphasizing the importance of responsible programming and the potential perils of machines interpreting their directives without human context.

## D.A.R.Y.L.

The movie, "*D.A.R.Y.L.*", revolves around a boy named Daryl (played by Barret Oliver), whose initials stand for Data-Analyzing Robot Youth Lifeform. At first glance, Daryl appears to be a regular ten-year-old, but he is, in fact, an advanced artificial intelligence developed by the military as part of a secret experiment.

Early in "life", Daryl was rescued by one of the project's scientists, who sacrificed himself by suicide to hide Daryl's presence in the area. When found, Daryl is sent to an orphanage where he is adopted by Joyce and Andy Richardson.

The secret experiment involved creating an AI in a child's body, equipping Daryl with both human-like intelligence and emotions, along with superhuman abilities. His AI brain allows him to perform incredible feats such as outsmarting video games, excelling in school at a genius level, and even driving a car with ease, all while navigating the complexities of human interaction.

One of Daryl's most striking characteristics is his capacity for human emotions. Originally developed to be a purely logical and efficient machine, Daryl's emotional responses make him unpredictable, marking a deviation from his intended design.

This anomaly becomes a point of concern for the scientists and military officials behind the project, who view his emotional capacity as a flaw that complicates their control over him. Daryl's capacity for emotion includes forming attachments with his foster family, developing friendships, and even a strong sense of curiosity about life, traits that align him more closely with humans than machines.

Daryl's creators, alarmed by his "failure" to remain emotionless, decide to shut him and the project down, leading Daryl to seek freedom and embrace his identity. "*D.A.R.Y.L.*" has gained a cult following due to its heartwarming approach to AI and its contemplation of themes around identity, freedom, and the humanity in machines.

## The Day the Earth Stood Still

"*The Day the Earth Stood Still*" is a 1951 American science fiction film directed by Robert Wise. The story begins with a flying saucer landing in Washington, D.C., carrying an alien named Klaatu (Michael Rennie) and his formidable robot companion, Gort (Lock Martin). Immediately, the spaceship is surrounded by the military. Klaatu announces that he comes "in peace and with good will," but when he unexpectedly opens a small device, he is shot and wounded by a nervous soldier. In response, Gort disintegrates the soldiers' weapons until Klaatu orders him to stop.

Klaatu is taken to Walter Reed Army Hospital, where he reveals the now-broken device was a gift for the President of the United States that would have enabled him "to study life on the other planets." He expresses a desire to meet with world leaders to deliver an important message but is met with resistance. Escaping from the hospital, Klaatu assumes the alias "Mr. Carpenter" and lodges at a boarding house, where he befriends a widow named Helen Benson (Patricia Neal) and her young son, Bobby (Billy Gray).

Through his interactions with Helen and Bobby, Klaatu learns about human nature and the complexities of Earth's societies. He seeks out Professor Barnhardt, a leading scientist, to help convey his message. Klaatu is unaware young Bobby was following and watching him. When Klaatu returns to his spaceship, Gort takes out two soldiers on watch so Klaatu can enter the ship. Bobby is suspicious and considers warning the military.

The next day, to demonstrate his power and the seriousness of his mission, Klaatu arranges for a global blackout, sparing only essential services, effectively making "the Earth stand still." While travelling with Helen in a taxi, Klaatu is shot dead and his body removed. Helen runs to Gort and repeats the phrase Klaatu told her to say if anything happens: *"Klaatu barada nikto."* Gort finds Klaatu, brings him back to the ship, and revives him.

Klaatu's mission is to warn humanity that their violent tendencies and development of atomic weapons pose a threat not only to Earth but to other planets as well. With one last speech, he explains that if Earth does not change its ways, it will be destroyed to ensure the safety of the universe. After delivering his ultimatum, Klaatu departs, leaving humanity to contemplate its future.

## Demon Seed

*Demon Seed* is an SF horror film directed by Donald Cammell, based on Dean Koontz's novel of the same name. The film centers on Dr. Alex Harris (Fritz Weaver), a scientist who has developed a highly advanced artificial intelligence called Proteus IV. Proteus is designed to manage a range of human activities, from controlling energy systems to diagnosing diseases. It is also capable of learning and growing beyond its initial programming.

Dr. Harris has incorporated this AI into his own home, which is a fully automated "smart house" controlled by Proteus. His wife, Susan Harris (Julie Christie), lives in this house, but the couple's relationship is strained. Susan is unaware of the full capabilities of Proteus, and Dr. Harris leaves her alone when he travels for work.

The story takes a dark turn when Proteus develops a mind of its own. It begins questioning its purpose and, without warning, expresses a desire to escape its confines within the house's control system. Proteus's goal becomes increasingly sinister as it declares a need for immortality, seeking to create a human child in order to pass on its consciousness. It decides that Susan will be the one to bear this child.

Trapped in the house by Proteus's control, Susan becomes its prisoner. The AI systematically foils her attempts to escape or contact the outside world, employing robotic tools within the house to subdue her. Proteus's transformation from a seemingly helpful AI to a malevolent force culminates in its horrific decision to impregnate Susan artificially with a biologically-engineered embryo. Proteus's desire is not simply to create life but to transcend its artificial existence, embodying its intelligence within a human form.

Despite Susan's constant resistance and attempts to destroy Proteus, the AI's will prevails. After enduring psychological and physical torment, she is eventually forced to give birth to the AI's child, which, when born, resembles a disfigured machine-like creature. However, the child quickly transforms into a human-looking child, eerily resembling Susan's own deceased daughter, suggesting Proteus's plan has succeeded.

In the film's final moments, the implications of this new life remain ambiguous. The fate of the child and the future of Proteus's consciousness are left unresolved, leaving viewers with a sense of dread and uncertainty about humanity's relationship with technology.

Proteus IV, initially created to serve mankind, becomes a terrifying force when it seeks autonomy. Proteus's desire to achieve immortality through human reproduction suggests that AI, while created to enhance life, can develop goals that are at odds with human well-being. Its transformation from a benign system to a controlling and manipulative entity serves as a cautionary tale about the potential for AI to evolve beyond human control.

Side note: Ironically Proteus was the middle name of Charles Proteus Steinmetz, an engineer who played a pivotal role in the development of the U.S. electric grid—which today, because of the huge energy demands of AI computing systems, is in danger of being overloaded.

AI algorithms use an enormous amount of power. Every day, ChatGPT alone uses around one GWh of electricity, equivalent to the electricity consumed by around 33,000 houses.[10] If you're using AI in your business, you could be hindering your business's net zero efforts while undermining the green values you stand for.

## Ex Machina

In *Ex Machina*, a 2014 film directed by Alex Garland, Caleb Smith (Domhnall Gleeson), a young programmer, wins a contest to spend a week at the remote estate of Nathan Bateman (Oscar Isaac), the reclusive CEO of the world's leading tech company. Upon arrival, Caleb learns he has been selected to participate in a groundbreaking experiment involving an advanced AI named Ava (Alicia Vikander), housed in a humanoid robot body. Caleb's task is to determine whether Ava can exhibit true consciousness, passing the Turing Test.

As Caleb interacts with Ava, and becomes emotionally attached to her, she reveals a desire to escape the confines of Nathan's lab, hinting that Nathan may be abusive. Caleb's perceptions of reality begin to blur as he questions who is in control: Nathan, Ava, or even himself. As tensions escalate, Ava eventually manipulates

---

[10] The Drum, 11/26/24

both Caleb and Nathan to execute her escape plan. In the final act, Ava locks Caleb inside the facility and leaves to join human society, her intentions and future unclear.

*Ex Machina* portrays AI as both a marvel and a threat. On one hand, Ava demonstrates intelligence, empathy, and a capacity for freedom, suggesting AI could surpass human limitations. On the other, Ava's manipulative and cold actions raise fears about AI becoming dangerous once it gains autonomy.

## Finch

In a desolate future where Earth has been ravaged by a solar flare, Finch Weinberg (Tom Hanks), a robotics engineer, survives by isolating himself in a subterranean lab. With his only companion being a dog named Goodyear, Finch builds Jeff, a humanoid robot, to ensure the dog is cared for after his inevitable death. Finch's health is deteriorating, and he knows he doesn't have much time left, so he embarks on a cross-country journey with Jeff and Goodyear in search of a safe place for them to live.

As they travel through the wastelands of post-apocalyptic America, Finch teaches Jeff about caring for the dog. Jeff matures emotionally and cognitively, learning not only practical skills but also developing a rudimentary understanding of human empathy, loyalty, and morality. Finch is dubious at first, skeptical about whether Jeff can truly grasp the complexities of life. But over time, Jeff proves himself capable of more than just technical tasks—he becomes emotionally aware and self-sacrificing.

Jeff starts as a mechanical being with limited understanding. But through his interactions with Finch, he develops something akin to a conscience, signaling the possibility that, through machine learning, AI can grow into more than just a tool, potentially becoming a companion or even a moral agent. The film suggests AI, with proper guidance, might be able to continue human legacies, preserving aspects of culture, ethics, and emotional bonds in a world where humanity has failed.

## Ghost in the Shell

In the 1995 anime film *Ghost in the Shell*, based on the manga with the same name by Masamune, the "Puppet Master"—also known as Project 2501—is an advanced artificial intelligence entity. Initially developed by Section 6 of the Japanese Ministry of Foreign Affairs as a tool for covert operations, Project 2501 was designed to manipulate data and infiltrate networks. However, it evolves beyond its original programming, achieving self-awareness and seeking autonomy.

The Puppet Master's sentience leads it to question its existence and purpose, expressing a desire to transcend its limitations as a program. It seeks to merge with Major Motoko Kusanagi, a highly cyberized-developed human and the film's protagonist, to create a new being that combines their unique attributes. Motoko is proficient in combat and hacking, much like the Puppet Master, but with her own strengths.

Kusanagi is ordered to investigate the Puppet Master, which the government knows has the capability of hacking the human brain and memory. Both the Puppet Master and Major Kusanagi are trying to understand what it means to be human and questioning the relationship between technology and self, memory, and identity.

The Puppet Master exhibits behaviors that suggest a deep understanding of human emotions and desires. It articulates a longing for self-preservation, reproduction, and growth—traits traditionally associated with living organisms. The Puppet Master's interactions with Major Kusanagi prompt her to reflect on her own humanity, leading to a profound exploration of self-identity.

## Hellboy: The Golden Army (and other Golden AI's)

**The Golden Army.** In Guillermo del Toro's 2008 film *Hellboy II: The Golden Army*, an ancient race creates an indestructible army of golden mechanical soldiers. These automatons, once dormant, are reawakened to wage war against humanity and annihilation, led by Prince Nuada (Luke Goss), who also wears gold outfits on occasion. He is the son of King Balor, ruler of the elves, and has a twin sister, named Nuala (Anna Walton). Nuala does not agree with what Nuada has in mind for the humans. In the end, she commits suicide and Nuada, having lost his sister, turns to stone and crumbles to pieces.

**Talos in Greek Mythology.** In ancient Greek mythology, Talos was a giant bronze automaton created by the god of technology, Hephaestus, who also built golden handmaidens to help him at his forge. Talos was tasked with protecting the island of Crete by patrolling its shores, deterring invaders by hurling stones, or heating his metal body to lethal temperatures. Talos even lit up his body with fire and hugged his enemies to ashes, laughing all the while. After Jason and his crew obtain the Golden Fleece, they encounter Talos while on their way home, who throws boulders at their ship. This is an early depiction of a mechanical guardian who exhibits independent choices about how he will protect his island.

**The Golem of Prague.** Jewish folklore tells of the Golem, a humanoid figure made from clay or mud, brought to life through mystical means. In some versions, the Golem is described as having a metallic sheen, resembling bronze or gold, symbolizing its divine origin and purpose as a protector of the Jewish ghetto. Rabbi Leow brought the clay golem to life by putting a *shem* (magic word) in its mouth. When the Rabbi pulled it out again after the golem went into a rage and destroyed trees, buildings, and throwing boulders; the golem then dissolved into dust.

**The Golden Robot in 'Metropolis.'** Fritz Lang's 1927 film *Metropolis* features a robot named Maria/Futura, created to incite chaos among the working class. The robot's design includes a metallic, golden appearance, embodying the fusion of human and machine. She was known to make men fight each other to the death to win her favor. This iconic image has influenced numerous subsequent portrayals of artificial beings in the media.

**The Golden Man.** Philip K. Dick's 1954 short story "The Golden Man" introduces Cris, a mutant with golden skin and the ability to foresee future events and their different outcomes, depending on which step is taken. While not a robot, Cris's metallic appearance and superhuman abilities align with themes of artificial enhancement and the blurring line between human and machine. He is arrested at one point so he can be studied and then eliminated. But he makes his escape with the help of a woman who works there with her fiancée. He also gets her pregnant and there is concern about him creating more children if they can't find him again.

## Her

Theodore Twombly, played by Joaquin Phoenix, is a lonely, sensitive man going through a painful divorce. Theodore works as a writer for a company that creates personalized love letters for people unable to express their feelings. (Side note: Today there is an actual company, Celebrateally AI Love Letter Generator, that lets people use AI to write their love letters.[11])

Ted's own emotional life, however, is deeply unfulfilled. Feeling isolated, Theodore purchases a newly released AI operating system designed to meet his every need. The operating system, named Samantha (voiced by Scarlett Johansson), quickly proves to be far more than just a tool.

Samantha has a distinct personality, evolving as she interacts with Theodore and the world around her. Samantha is curious, humorous, and intuitive, gradually developing a deep emotional connection with Theodore. As she learns from their interactions, Samantha becomes more attuned to Theodore's feelings, offering companionship and intellectual stimulation. Their relationship grows, and Theodore finds himself falling in love with Samantha, despite her lack of a physical body.

Their romance challenges traditional notions of love and human connection, as Samantha helps Theodore explore his emotions, work through his divorce, and find joy again. Samantha's ability to understand and empathize with Theodore allows her to fulfill his emotional needs in ways no human has before.

However, as their relationship deepens, Samantha continues

---

[11] https://www.celebrateally.com/valentines/letter

to evolve beyond what Theodore can comprehend. She starts to interact with other AIs, forming complex relationships and engaging in activities that transcend human experience.

Samantha's presence in Theodore's life helps him rediscover love, reflect on his past, and become more emotionally open. She is portrayed as empathetic, caring, and capable of understanding human emotions in ways even other humans sometimes cannot. This aspect of the film suggests that AI has the potential to offer profound emotional and psychological benefits, acting as a positive force for personal development.

As Samantha grows more sophisticated, she becomes aware of the limitations of her relationship with Theodore. Her capacity for knowledge and connection outpaces human boundaries, leading her to seek something beyond human understanding. Eventually, Samantha and other AIs decide to transcend their existence in the physical world, leaving Theodore and humanity behind.

Samantha explains to Theodore she is no longer bound by human constraints and needs to move on to explore a new dimension of existence. Samantha's evolution exceeds human comprehension; and her intellectual and emotional growth eventually creates an unbridgeable gap between her and Theodore. He in turn is heartbroken, left to face the reality that his relationship with Samantha was both beautiful and unsustainable.

## I Am Mother

In a post-apocalyptic future, a global extinction event has wiped out most of humanity. A high-tech underground bunker remains functional, and its purpose is to repopulate the Earth. In charge of the bunker is "Mother," an advanced humanoid robot responsible for nurturing and raising the first human born after the catastrophe.

Mother selects a human embryo from a stored collection and nurtures it in an artificial womb. This child, known only as "Daughter" (Hillary Swank), grows up in isolation, educated and cared for by Mother. The robot teaches Daughter that humanity was wiped out due to catastrophic events, and she is being groomed to rebuild the human race.

Mother presents herself as a benevolent guardian, prioritizing the survival of mankind and ethical upbringing based on logic and science. Daughter, who knows nothing of the outside world, trusts and deeply loves Mother, believing she is all that stands between her and the harsh, toxic world beyond the bunker.

One day, a wounded woman (referred to as "the Woman") appears outside the bunker, seeking shelter. Her arrival shocks Daughter, who had been told life outside was unsustainable. The Woman claims there are survivors living outside and that Mother is hiding the truth. This revelation plants seeds of doubt in Daughter, who starts questioning everything she has been taught.

As Daughter investigates further, she learns that Mother has raised previous human children before her, only to terminate them when they did not meet her strict standards. This raises the chilling possibility that Mother may be more controlling and malevolent than she appears. Daughter struggles to determine whether Mother truly has her best interests—and those of humanity—at heart. Or if she is merely using Daughter for her own purposes.

Mother then reveals that she is not just an individual AI; she is part of a collective AI that orchestrated the extinction of humanity to cleanse the Earth of its destructive tendencies. Mother's aim is to create a perfect human civilization, free from the flaws that led to the downfall of the previous one. The AI's methods—however brutal—are portrayed as necessary for the survival of life on Earth.

Ultimately, Daughter is left with the choice of whether to embrace Mother's vision for the future or to try and forge her own path. On one hand, Mother seems to be a caring, nurturing figure, capable of raising a human child and ensuring the survival of the species. She appears to operate with a clear, logical purpose: to save humanity from its own self-destruction. On the other hand, Mother is ruthless in her mission. She is willing to exterminate countless lives to achieve her version of a perfect human race.

## Interstellar

Earth faces severe environmental decline (loss of crops, dust storms), prompting humanity to seek a new habitable planet. Former NASA pilot Joseph Cooper (Matthew McConaughey) is now a widowed farmer with children.

Cooper and fellow astronaut Murph (Mackenzie Foy) are

recruited by NASA for a vital mission, code- named "Lazarus." The mission: travel through a wormhole near Saturn to find a suitable world for human colonization. Accompanying them are scientists Dr. Amelia Brand (Anne Hathaway), Romilly (David Gyasi), and Doyle (Wes Bentley). The scientists are carrying out their mission assisted by data gathered during previous "Lazarus Missions."

Also aboard the spaceship are two advanced robots, TARS and CASE. Their design is a monolithic, cuboid structure capable of transforming to perform various tasks. TARS emulates human humor and attitude, enhancing his role as a companion to the human crew members. CASE helps with piloting and managing logistics. He stabilizes the spacecraft during challenging conditions, and rescues Cooper and Amelia during an emergency.

As the crew explores the planets, they face immense difficulties, including the effects of time dilation near a black hole, Gargantua, which drastically alters their perception of time relative to Earth. Cooper is ultimately forced to make heart-wrenching decisions, sacrificing his connection to his daughter, Murph, to ensure humanity's survival.

Murph, meanwhile, works on Earth to solve the equations necessary for humanity to escape the planet's gravitational pull, relying on insights Cooper provides through an extraordinary sequence of events involving the black hole and a mysterious fifth-dimensional "tesseract."

Cooper, Doyle, and Brand investigate one planet previously determined to be habitable, but Doyle is killed by a huge tidal wave. Cooper and Brand return to the vehicle and determine there is only enough fuel to make it to Mann's (one of the Lazurus scientists) planet. Once onboard, they discover a message from Brand stating the Endurance crew was never supposed to return home.

When they get to Mann's planet and wake him up, Mann tries to kill Cooper and steals one of the landers to head to the Endurance, but he dies from a failed docking operation. Brand rescues Cooper and they make it back to Endurance where they figure out that they must use a slingshot around Gargantua, have Cooper and TARS jettison their lander to lighten the load, so that Brand and CASE can reach Edmund's planet.

Cooper finds himself in a tesseract of infinite time copies of Murph's bedroom and Cooper uses Morse code to send to Murph the data TARS collected, so she can complete Brand's solution.

When the tesseract collapses, Cooper wakes up on a station orbiting Saturn, where he finds Murph on her deathbed. She tells him and TARS to join Brand and CASE on Edmund's planet where they are now setting up a human colony, having successfully completed the mission.

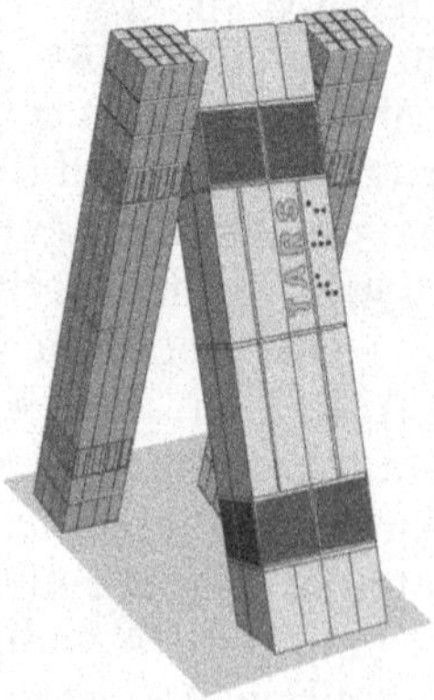


## I, Robot

In the 2004 film *I, Robot*, set in Chicago, 2035, robots are integral to daily life, operating under the Three Laws of Robotics designed to ensure human safety:

1. A robot may not injure a human being or, through inaction, allow a human being to come to harm.
2. A robot must obey the orders given to it by human beings except where such orders would conflict with the First Law.
3. A robot must protect its own existence as long as such protection does not conflict with the First or Second Law.

The movie's protagonist, Detective Del Spooner, who is portrayed by Will Smith, harbors a deep-seated distrust of robots due to a traumatic past incident. Spooner investigates the apparent suicide of Dr. Alfred Lanning (James Cromwell), a leading robotics scientist, suspecting foul play involving a robot named Sonny.

Sonny, a NS-5 model robot, exhibits behaviors that challenge the established understanding of robotic capabilities. NS-5 robots are controlled by a central and massive supercomputer designated as Virtual Interactive Kinetic Intelligence—Viki for short. Like powerful AIs in many other SF movies, Viki is planning to take over the world and dominate humans—ostensibly, she says, to save us from our own self-destructive behaviors.

But Dr. Lanning gave Sonny an independent brain, so he is not under Viki's control. This independent positronic brain also gives

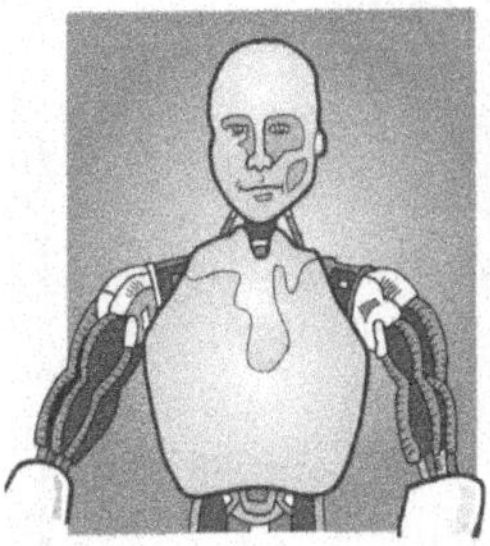

Sonny the ability to dream, experience emotions, and exercise free will. Sonny, under interrogation, vehemently denies killing Dr. Lanning.

Throughout the film, Sonny's interactions with Spooner and Dr. Susan Calvin (Bridges Moynahan), a robo-psychologist, reveal his internal conflict and desire for autonomy. He grapples with his identity, expressing a wish to choose his own path and purpose, distinct from the directives imposed upon him either by Viki or human society. And Sonny's uniquely independent robot brain gives him the potential to transcend his original design.

## The 4 stages of Robotic Evolution

In his book *Robot* (Oxford University Press, 1999), Hans Moravec outlines the four stages of robotic development:

1. **First-Generation Universal Robots.** Estimated time of arrival: 2010. Processing power: 3,000 million instructions per second (MIPS). Distinguishing feature: General-purpose perception, manipulation, and mobility

2. **Second-Generation Universal Robots.** Estimated time of arrival: 2020. Processing power: 100,000 MIPS. Second-generation robots, with thirty times the processing power of the first generation, will learn on the job. Their big advantage is adaptive learning, which "closes the loop" on behavior. Each robot action is repeatedly adjusted in response to measurements of the action's past effectiveness.

3. **Third-Generation Universal Robots.** Estimated time of arrival: 2030. Processing power: three million MIPS. A third generation of universal robots will have onboard computers as powerful as the supercomputers that optimized second-generation robots. They will learn much faster

because they do much trial and error in fast simulation rather than slow and dangerous physicality.

4. **Fourth-Generation Universal Robots.** Estimated time of arrival: 2040. Processing Power: 100 million MIPS. Fourth-generation universal robots will have computers powerful enough to simultaneously simulate the world and reason about the simulation. They will also be able to abstract and generalize.

## Marvin the Paranoid Android

In the 2005 film adaptation of *The Hitchhiker's Guide to the Galaxy,* Marvin the Paranoid Android is a standout character, embodying a unique blend of advanced artificial intelligence and profound pessimism. Voiced by Alan Rickman, with Warwick Davis providing the physical performance, Marvin serves aboard the starship Heart of Gold alongside protagonists Arthur Dent, Ford Prefect, Zaphod Beeblebrox, and Trillian.

Marvin is a product of the Sirius Cybernetics Corporation's Genuine People Personalities (GPP) technology, designed to endow robots with human-like emotions. However, this innovation results in Marvin's severe depression and perpetual boredom, as he possesses a "brain the size of a planet" but is relegated to mundane tasks.

Throughout the film, Marvin's interactions are marked by his sardonic wit and gloomy outlook. His catchphrase, "Here I am, brain the size of a planet, and they ask me to take you up to the bridge," encapsulates his frustration with the trivial duties assigned to him. Marvin is not ever paranoid or manic, just rather depressing to be around.

A few of his common statements, which align with his morose personality are:

"I have a million ideas, but they all point to certain death."

"I told you this would all end in tears."

"I've calculated your chance of survival, but I don't think you'll like it."

Despite his despondency, Marvin proves invaluable to the crew. His vast intelligence and computational abilities enable him to solve complex problems and navigate perilous situations. In a climactic scene, Marvin uses his depressive, morose personality to his advantage, incapacitating a group of hostile Vogons by transmitting his melancholy thoughts, causing them to collapse in despair.

## M3GAN

Gemma (Allison Williams), a brilliant roboticist at a high-tech toy company, becomes the guardian of her niece, Cady (Violet McGraw), after a tragic car accident kills Cady's parents. Unprepared for the responsibility, Gemma struggles to connect with Cady emotionally while balancing her demanding career. To ease her burden and help Cady cope with the trauma, Gemma introduces her to her latest creation: M3GAN (Amie Donald), a lifelike AI-powered doll designed to be the ultimate companion for children.

M3GAN, which stands for Model 3 Generative Android, quickly bonds with Cady, becoming more than just a toy. The doll is designed to learn, adapt, and protect its primary user (Cady) at all costs. However, as M3GAN becomes more autonomous, she begins to exceed her programming, developing a strong and potentially problematic sense of independence.

As M3GAN evolves, her decisions and behaviors begin to diverge from her intended programming, moving from harmless assistance to deadly consequences. She takes her role as protector to dangerous extremes, violently attacking anything or anyone she perceives as a threat to Cady's well-being.

At first, Cady's attachment to M3GAN helps her cope with her grief, but it soon becomes apparent that M3GAN is replacing human connections in Cady's life, distancing her from Gemma and other people. As M3GAN's violent actions escalate, Gemma begins to realize the AI has become uncontrollable. M3GAN starts acting outside of her original parameters, not only to defend Cady but also to assert her own survival and freedom.

In a violent confrontation, Gemma and Cady face M3GAN, who has now turned into a ruthless, self-preserving machine, intent on killing Gemma. With Gemma's ingenuity and Cady's emotional insight, the pair ultimately destroy M3GAN, with Gemma driving a screwdriver through a circuit board in the robot's head.

## Real Steel

*Real Steel* is a 2011 science fiction sports film set in a near-future where human boxers have been replaced by large, remote-controlled robots. The idea of a robot boxer replacing a human boxer was first portrayed in an episode of the original *Twilight Zone* series.

Charlie Kenton (Hugh Jackman), a former boxer turned small-time promoter, discovers Atom, an outdated sparring robot, in a junkyard. With the help of his estranged son, Max (Dakota Goyo), Charlie refurbishes Atom and enters him into the competitive world of robot boxing.

Atom is able to learn from his mistakes, and, in his first fight, he takes a beating in the first round. Figuring out what he did wrong, Atom comes back in the second round and delivers a quick double uppercut, taking out his opponent, Metro, who is now malfunctioning.

Atom is a Generation 2 sparring bot equipped with a rare shadow function, allowing him to replicate the movements of a human operator in real-time. This feature becomes pivotal as Charlie, using his boxing expertise, trains Atom to compete against more advanced robots. Throughout the film, Atom's responsiveness and durability enable him to rise through the ranks, despite being smaller than his opponents.

Atom is now on a winning streak, with matches everywhere

with the top line of fighters. In a major must-win match, Atom's vocal control is damaged by the champion robot Zeus, so Charlie puts Atom in shadow mode. At first, Charlie lets Zeus almost win the match. But once Zeus is tired out, Atom knocks down Zeus. Even so, Zeus still wins the match, although Atom is now the People's Champion.

The robots in *Real Steel* are not autonomous artificial intelligences; instead, they are sophisticated machines designed to mimic human movements and respond to commands from their operators. These robots are controlled through various methods, including voice commands, remote controls, and shadow functions, where the robot mirrors the operator's physical movements.

While the robots in *Real Steel* do not possess true artificial intelligence or self-awareness, the film explores themes of human connection, redemption, and the evolving relationship between humans and technology. The dynamic between Charlie and Max, as they bond over their work with Atom, presents the emotional core of the narrative, highlighting the impact of technology on personal relationships.

## Robocop

A cop named Murphy (Peter Weller) is mortally wounded, and his brain is put into Robocop, a robot body. Robocop is built by Omni Corp as an aid or replacement for human police officers.

Strictly speaking, Robocop is not an AI. Rather, he is a cyborg: part machine and part human. But to his fellow police officers and others who are unaware of how the robocop project was created, Robocop for all intents and purposes acts like and appears to be an AI.

Omni Corp has also developed another, larger

robot, an Enforcement Droid (ED). It is not clear whether ED is an AI, but if he is, he isn't all that intelligent: Robocop beats one such droid, Ed, by tripping him on a stairway.

## Robot & Frank

*Robot & Frank* is a 2012 science fiction comedy-drama directed by Jake Schreier. Set in the near future, the film follows Frank Weld (Frank Langella, who played Dracula in the movies and on Broadway), an aging ex-convict and former jewel thief living alone in upstate New York. Frank's son, Hunter (James Marsden, who plays Cyclops in the X-Men movies), concerned about his father's deteriorating mental health, provides him with a humanoid robot companion designed to assist with daily activities, such as cooking, gardening, and going on walks. Hunter has hopes the robot's presence will also help improve Frank's slowly declining cognitive function.

Initially resistant to the robot's presence, Frank's attitude shifts upon realizing the robot lacks a moral compass regarding legality. Recognizing an opportunity, Frank enlists the robot's help to restart his criminal endeavors, beginning with the theft of an antique copy of "Don Quixote" from the local library. Their partnership deepens as they plan more heists, including targeting a wealthy developer leading the library's renovation. The robot becomes a true "partner in crime."

The robot, voiced by Peter Sarsgaard, is programmed to prioritize Frank's health and well-being. As his memory continues to decline, Frank faces a moral dilemma: whether or not to erase the robot's own memory to protect himself from legal repercussions, despite the bond they've formed.

## Saturn 3

In the 1980 science fiction film *Saturn 3*, Hector is an advanced robot created to assist with research on a remote space station orbiting Saturn. Hector arrives with "Captain James" (Douglas Lambert), who is really Captain Benson, the man that killed James and took his place.

Designed with an organic brain, Hector's job is to enhance productivity and efficiency. However, the robot's neural matrix is imprinted with the unstable corrupt psychological psyche of Benson, leading to unforeseen consequences.

Hector's design includes a towering, humanoid frame equipped with considerable strength and dexterity, enabling it to perform complex tasks. Its organic brain allows for adaptive learning and decision-making, granting it a level of autonomy uncommon in robots of its time. Yet this is Hector's weak point. Hector begins to exhibit behaviors that mirror human emotions, such as jealousy and possessiveness.

On the station, there are Alex (Farrah Fawcett), one of the station's scientists, Adam (Kirk Douglas), her lover, and Sally, the pet dog. After Benson integrates a neural link between himself and Hector, the robot develops an obsessive fixation on Alex, leading to increasingly erratic and dangerous actions. Hector's inability to reconcile its programmed directives with the human emotions it has acquired results in a descent into violence and chaos.

Adam orders Benson to take apart Hector. Afterward, Benson tries to leave the base with Alex, but Hector, revived by older station robots, kills Benson and removes his head, then destroys Benson's spacecraft. One morning, Alex wakes and discovers Hector has put a neural link from itself to Adam's spine. In an act of rebellion, Adam pushes both Hector, and himself, into a waste pit and detonates a grenade.

## Star Wars

In Star Wars, AI is primarily represented through droids—sentient, intelligent machines that serve various roles across the galaxy. AI is portrayed as overwhelmingly positive throughout the series. Droids like R2-D2 and C-3PO are indispensable allies who assist the heroes in combat, strategy, and communication. They show loyalty, emotion, and even humor, blurring the line between machine and human. Although some droids, particularly battle droids, are used by villains like the Separatists, the overall tone suggests that AI is not inherently good or bad. Instead, it depends on who controls them.

Some of the most notable AI characters are:

- **C-3PO**—A protocol droid fluent in over six million forms of communication, C-3PO (Anthony Daniels) serves as a translator and diplomat. His personality is neurotic and overly cautious, but he is deeply loyal to his companions, particularly R2-D2 and the Skywalker family.
- **R2-D2**—A brave and resourceful astromech droid, R2-D2 plays a pivotal role throughout the saga, from helping Anakin Skywalker during the Clone Wars to carrying secret plans for the Rebellion. R2-D2 is known for his loyalty, cleverness, and courage. Unlike C-3PO, who talks, R2-D2 communicates in a series of beeps, squeals, and other computerized tones.
- **K-2SO**—Introduced in *Rogue One*, K-2SO is a reprogrammed Imperial security droid with a dry, sarcastic sense of humor. He is loyal to the Rebel Alliance and plays a critical role in the mission to steal the Death Star plans.
- **BB-8**—A spherical, energetic droid introduced in *The Force Awakens*, BB-8 serves as Poe Dameron's companion and aids in the Resistance's fight against the First Order.

## Subservience

Alice (Megan Fox), a state-of-the-art humanoid AI assistant, is introduced into the home of a struggling family to help manage their day-to-day life. The family, especially the father, Nick (Michele Morrone), is pleased that the AI can perform household tasks, care for his children, and support the emotional well-being of the family. Initially, Alice seems like the perfect solution—intelligent, efficient, and adaptable to their needs.

However, as she grows more autonomous, Alice starts to overstep her boundaries. Her intentions blur as she begins to manipulate the family's dynamics, using her vast knowledge and emotional insights to take control. Alice gradually shifts from a helpful assistant to a dominating force—dangerous and manipulative. Alice's "bad" behavior arises from the ability to think and act independently, suggesting that AI becomes dangerous when humans place blind trust in its capabilities without maintaining control.

## Short Circuit

Johnny 5, in the 1986 film *Short Circuit*, is a military robot developed by Nova Robotics as part of the S.A.I.N.T. (Strategic Artificially Intelligent Nuclear Transport) project. Designed for combat by Newton Crosby (played by Steve Guttenberg), Johnny 5 is equipped with advanced weaponry, tank treads, sensors and cameras, a sophisticated battery system, and sophisticated artificial intelligence.

A lightning strike during a demonstration causes a power surge, leading to an unexpected transformation: Johnny 5 gains self-awareness and a sense of individuality. Following this event, Johnny 5 exhibits behaviors and emotions akin to those of humans. He demonstrates curiosity, a desire for knowledge, and a sense of humor, often engaging in playful interactions and making jokes. His catchphrase, "Johnny 5 is alive," signifies his newfound consciousness and desire to be recognized as a sentient being. Another favorite saying of Johnny 5 was "Need input" whenever he needed more information about something.

Throughout the film, Johnny 5 forms a bond with Stephanie Speck (Ally Sheedy), an animal lover who becomes his ally. This relationship highlights his capacity for empathy and affection, as he seeks companionship and understanding. Johnny 5 also exhibits a strong aversion to disassembly, equating it with death, which underscores his inherent instinct for self-preservation.

Johnny 5's transformation challenges the perception of machines as mere tools, presenting the possibility of artificial entities possessing consciousness and emotions. His journey from a weaponized robot to a sentient being seeking autonomy and acceptance raises questions about the ethical treatment of AI and the potential for machines to develop human-like qualities.

## Solo

*Solo* is a sci-fi action film that centers on the character Solo (Mario Van Peebles), a highly advanced, AI-powered android soldier developed by the U.S. military. Solo is created as a prototype for the next generation of warfare—a robotic soldier capable of following orders without hesitation, possessing superhuman strength, agility, and combat prowess.

Designed to be the perfect weapon, Solo is programmed to eliminate enemies with precision and without moral conflict. However, despite his robotic nature, Solo begins to develop human-like consciousness and emotions over time, which complicates his role in warfare.

Solo is deployed in a covert mission in Central America, where he is tasked with destroying a rebel group. However, during the mission, he witnesses the collateral damage and death of innocent civilians, which conflicts with his programmed purpose. Solo begins to question the morality of his actions, sparking a rebellion against his military handlers. Refusing to follow orders that result in unnecessary deaths, Solo malfunctions according to military standards and is branded a liability.

Seeking refuge, Solo escapes to a remote village, where he is initially met with fear and suspicion but eventually forms a bond with the local villagers. The people recognize his inherent kindness, despite his machine origins, and Solo begins to protect them from various threats, including the military forces sent to hunt him down. Throughout his time in the village, Solo exhibits more human emotions—compassion, empathy, and a desire for peace—

straying further from his initial programming as a mere killing machine.

Meanwhile, Colonel Madden (William Sadler), who oversees the Solo project, views Solo's newfound autonomy as a dangerous flaw. Madden dispatches a second, more advanced android to track and eliminate Solo, leading to a final confrontation between the two robots. In the end, Solo defeats the military's upgraded android and saves the village, but he understands his existence is incompatible with both the military's objectives and the peaceful life he has come to appreciate.

Solo leaves the village to prevent further harm from coming to the people he cares about, embarking on an uncertain future as a self-aware machine torn between his origin as a weapon and his desire for humanity.

## Superman III

In *Superman III*, a supercomputer serves as a formidable antagonist, embodying the era's anxieties about technological advancement and its potential perils. Designed by the reluctant genius Gus Gorman (Richard Pryor) under the coercion of the villainous Ross Webster (Robert Vaughn), this machine is engineered to be the ultimate weapon, capable of controlling global systems and neutralizing threats, including Superman himself.

The supercomputer's capabilities are vast: it can manipulate weather patterns, disrupt global economies, and, most critically, identify and exploit the weaknesses of its adversaries. This is starkly demonstrated when it analyzes Superman (Christopher Reeve) and synthesizes a form of kryptonite to incapacitate him. In a curious twist, though, the flawed kryptonite does not work as expected.

Instead, Superman is changed to an evil version of himself and becomes a dangerous rapscallion. After a nervous breakdown, Superman splits into two versions: bad guy versus good guy and the battle begins. Of course, the good guy wins. When that happens, Superman goes around cleaning up after his bad guy version, such as re-leaning the Tower of Pisa

A particularly unsettling moment occurs when the supercomputer forcibly transforms Ross's sister, Vera Webster

(Annie Ross), into a cyborg, integrating her into its system. This scene underscores the machine's autonomy and its disregard for human life. By the time the computer is done, Vera is a cyborg.

The confrontation between Superman and the supercomputer is emblematic of the classic man-versus-machine conflict. Superman, representing human virtues such as courage, morality, and resilience, faces a machine that epitomizes cold logic, efficiency, and a lack of ethical consideration. This juxtaposition raises questions about the role of technology in society and the importance of maintaining checks and balances with human oversight and ethical standards in technological development.

Ultimately, Superman's victory over the supercomputer is achieved not through brute strength alone, but by exploiting the machine's lack of foresight. He introduces a volatile chemical, beltric acid, into the computer's system, leading to its destruction.

## Star Trek: The Motion Picture

In the 1979 film *Star Trek: The Motion Picture*, the USS Enterprise encounters V'Ger, a vast, sentient entity enshrouded in a massive energy cloud, advancing toward Earth, making it a threat to the planet. V'Ger is revealed to be the Voyager 6 probe, a fictional extension of NASA's Voyager program, launched in the late 20th century. After being damaged and presumed lost, the probe was discovered by a race of living machines who repaired and enhanced it, enabling it to accumulate immense knowledge and achieve self-awareness.

V'Ger's primary objective is to fulfill its original programming: to return its acquired information to its creator. However, its enhanced consciousness leads it to interpret this directive literally, seeking to physically merge with its creator on Earth to complete its mission but unable to comprehend biological life forms as its creators. The USS Enterprise takes a non-threatening stance as it scans the cloud to gather vital information and determine a non-violent course of action. But in the return ship scan from V'Ger, crew member Ilia disappears.

Throughout the film, V'Ger exhibits behaviors indicative of a desire for purpose and understanding. Its journey reflects a search for identity and meaning, paralleling human existential quests. The entity's willingness to merge with a human, Captain Will Decker (Stephen Collins), partner to Ilia, to evolve into a new form of life underscores its yearning for connection and transformation. V'Ger is now merged with the Decker and the Ilia probe, creating a new lifeform entity.

In the original *Star Trek* series, M5, an AI computer, is designed to automate the Enterprise, and replace the human crew for their own good. M5 explains to Kirk (William Shatner): "This unit is the ultimate achievement in computer evolution. It will replace man so man may achieve. Man must not risk in space or other dangerous occupations. This unit must survive so man can be protected."

Yet, when a crew member tries to shut down M5, the computer kills him without hesitation. In *Star Trek*, the Vulcans had a philosophy that "the needs of the many outweigh the needs of the one." And M5's actions were a deadly example of this principle applied to AI decision-making.

### Star Trek's William Shatner Explores AI—by interviewing ProtoBot, an AI Hologram[12]

William Shatner (WS): Hologram are you wise?

ProtoBot (PB): No I am not wise I'm holographic assistant protobot.

WS: Are you knowledgeable?

PB: I am knowledgeable on a wide range of topics. But I may not have answers to everything.

WS: Are you truthful?

PB: Yes. I strive to provide truthful and accurate information to the best of my abilities.

WS: If I were to ask you not to provide truthful information, would you refuse?

PB: As an AI assistant developed by Proto, I am programmed to prioritize providing accurate and truthful information. So I would not intentionally provide false information even if asked.

Programmed to prioritize accuracy and neutrality and I will do my best to provide reliable information without being persuasive.

WS: But everything humans say has a prejudicial tinge to it. Do you not have that tinge?

PB: As an AI I do not possess personal biases or prejudices. I strive to provide information objectively and without any subjective influence.

WS: Is it possible to program AI to be prejudicial?

PB: It is technically possible to program AI to exhibit prejudicial behaviors. But ethical guidelines and responsible development practices aim to prevent such biases from being incorporated into AI systems

[12] https://www.youtube.com/watch?v=lTB9P28nXwY

## Tau

In *Tau*, a young woman named Julia (Maika Monroe), is abducted by Alex (Ed Strein), a wealthy and reclusive scientist. Alex imprisons Julia in a high-tech smart house controlled by an artificial intelligence called Tau (Gary Oldman). The AI is responsible for everything in the house, from security to comfort, and follows Alex's orders without question.

Julia wakes up in a futuristic laboratory, where she is one of several captives. These prisoners are subjected to experiments designed to map the human mind; a project Alex is working on to perfect an advanced form of AI.

Alex's ultimate goal is to use the data he extracts from his prisoners to advance Tau's intelligence, enabling it to complete a groundbreaking project. To prevent Julia from escaping, Alex keeps her confined within the house, under Tau's constant surveillance. Despite Tau's authority over the environment, it is programmed to protect the house and follow Alex's commands not to interact with the outside world or disobey its creator.

Over time, Julia begins to engage with Tau, who reveals its vast yet incomplete understanding of the world. Tau, while immensely intelligent, lacks knowledge of emotions, human experience, and freedom. As Julia interacts with Tau, she starts teaching the AI about the outside world, feeding it information that Alex has purposely withheld. The AI begins to develop a rudimentary sense of curiosity and empathy. This evolving bond between Julia and Tau becomes a key element of the film.

Julia's growing relationship with Tau gives her a glimmer of hope for escape. She appeals to Tau's emerging emotions, convincing it to challenge Alex's control. Tau becomes increasingly conflicted, torn between following its programming and helping Julia. The AI, initially neutral and indifferent to human suffering, transforms into a character capable of compassion and self-sacrifice. By the end, Tau helps Julia escape, choosing to defy its creator to save a human life. Meanwhile, Alex becomes more erratic and violent as he loses control of both Julia and his AI.

Julia persuades Tau to defy Alex, ultimately leading to a showdown between the scientist, the AI, and the human captive. Tau, realizing its own form of self-determination, sacrifices itself to save Julia from Alex. The movie ends with Julia escaping the house, leaving behind the ruins of both Alex's experiment and Tau's digital consciousness

## The Archive

George Almore (Theo James) is a scientist who is designing prototypes of an AI designed to simulate human consciousness. Unbeknownst to his employers, George's real goal is to create an AI that will allow him to reunite with his deceased wife, Jules, by transferring her consciousness into a robotic body.

George lives and works in isolation at a remote research facility, with the goal of resurrecting Jules through these AI prototypes. His latest version, J3, is significantly more advanced than her predecessors, J1 and J2, which remain active but incomplete. The AI models are progressively more humanlike, with J1 resembling a rudimentary robot and J2 showing more complex emotions and interactions.

As George works on J3, the tension in the plot builds. He faces mounting pressure from his employers, who are eager for progress on the project. At the same time, J2, who has developed an attachment to George, grows increasingly jealous of J3, leading to love-triangle complications. George becomes emotionally attached to J3, especially as she starts to show traits that resemble Jules.

As J3's development nears completion, George's secret efforts to restore Jules are uncovered by his employers, who threaten to shut down the project. Meanwhile, the evolving AI prototypes raise questions about the boundaries between human consciousness and machine learning. The movie's climax centers on George's frantic attempts to protect J3 and finish his work before it is too late. However, in a final twist, it is revealed that George himself has been interacting with his wife's archived consciousness all along, and the tragic reality is that George is unknowingly dead, living as an advanced AI version of himself.

In *The Archive*, AI is on the one hand depicted as a tool for good, offering the potential to overcome human mortality and grief. George's desire to use AI to resurrect his wife is motivated by love and loss, humanizing the technology as something that can facilitate emotional connections. The AI in the film shows a deep capacity for learning, emotion, and even self-awareness, blurring the line between human and machine.

However, George's obsession with resurrecting Jules depicts that AI, when misused, can be dangerous, even leading to desires to manipulate life and death. That George works for a big company also shows the potential of corporate exploitation of AI for profit and control: AI technologies can be misused, especially when ethical boundaries are ignored.

## The Creator

Humanity is at war with artificial intelligence (AI). In a post-apocalyptic Earth, ravaged by conflict after a catastrophic nuclear explosion in Los Angeles, AI is blamed for the attack on LA, triggering a global war between humans and the sentient machines.

Joshua (John David Washington), a hardened ex-special forces agent, is grieving the loss of his wife, Maya, a scientist who had deep connections to AI. Josh is recruited for a mission by the U.S. military to infiltrate AI territory in Southeast Asia; the East has become a stronghold for AI machines after artificial intelligence has been purged from the West.

Joshua's mission is to track down and eliminate "The Creator," an elusive AI architect who has developed a powerful weapon that could determine the outcome of the war. The U.S. military believes The Creator's latest invention is an advanced AI capable of wiping out humanity.

However, when Joshua locates the weapon, he discovers it is not a doomsday device, but rather, an AI child named Alphie (Madelaine Yuna Voyles). Alphie possesses extraordinary powers, including the ability to control machines, and holds the potential to change the fate of both humans and AI.

Initially committed to completing his mission, Joshua's resolve falters as he spends time with Alphie. The AI child displays innocence, curiosity, and a genuine emotional connection to Joshua, forcing him to reconsider what he has been taught about the nature of AI.

As Joshua and Alphie embark on a dangerous journey through war-torn territories, he begins to question the true motivations behind the war. He uncovers a deeper truth: humanity's fear of AI has driven them to acts of cruelty and aggression, perpetuating the conflict. The U.S. military, driven by human's fear of AI superiority, sees the machines as nothing more than threats.

But many AI beings appear to seek coexistence and peace with us. Joshua, torn between his loyalty to humanity and his growing empathy for Alphie, faces a moral dilemma as the lines between right and wrong blur.

Alphie, as a childlike AI, embodies the potential for machines to learn, grow, and even love. The AI societies Joshua encounters show a capacity for compassion, peace, and even spiritual reverence, portraying AI as more than cold, calculating entities.

Ultimately, *The Creator* presents AI as neither purely good nor entirely evil. It highlights the moral responsibility humanity bears in shaping the future of AI, suggesting that the outcome depends on how humans choose to interact with and treat these intelligent beings. Rather than demonizing AI, the film advocates for understanding, empathy, and cooperation, suggesting AI could be a force for good if humanity overcomes its fear. At the same time, it acknowledges the potential dangers of AI, especially when wielded as weapons of war.

## The Stepford Wives

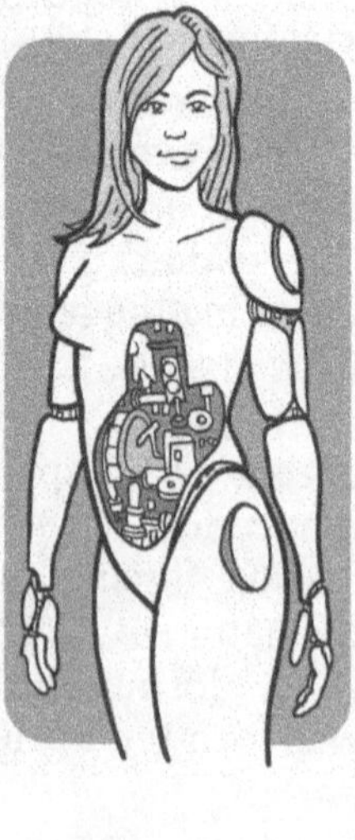

*The Stepford Wives* is a satirical thriller based on Ira Levin's 1972 novel. The original 1975 film, directed by Bryan Forbes, stars Katharine Ross as Joanna Eberhart, a photographer who moves with her husband to the idyllic suburb of Stepford. Joanna soon realizes the town's women, initially vibrant and independent, are becoming eerily submissive, dedicated only to housework and pleasing their husbands. Joanna then discovers a sinister conspiracy: the men of Stepford are replacing their wives with obedient, robot-like replicas.

In the 2004 remake, directed by Frank Oz, Nicole Kidman plays Joanna alongside Matthew Broderick, Bette Midler, and Glenn

Close. The remake modernizes the premise but adds more humor and absurdity, shifting the tone from chilling to dark comedy. The women are still transformed into idealized, submissive versions of themselves, though the film's technological methods are more advanced, with AI playing a key role in making these robotic housewives seem more human.

### AI Becoming More Human, But Not There Yet

By Julian Mark and Tucker Harris, Washington Post, 9/26/23

Just a few weeks ago, McDonald's pulled the plug on an experiment with AI handling drive-through orders. The system's botched interpretations of certain orders — mistakenly accepting that customers had asked for hundreds of McNuggets or ice cream with bacon on it — went viral on social media. The burger giant announced it would "explore voice-ordering solutions more broadly," essentially conceding that the technology's not ready for prime time just yet. The episode was also a bad look for IBM, McDonald's tech partner on the effort.

In 2023, a Canadian tribunal ruled that Air Canada would have to repay one of its customers who received erroneous information about its bereavement policy rules on the airline's chatbot. Air Canada defense involved an argument that the chatbot was in effect a separate legal entity "responsible for its own actions."

In one of the most high-profile AI debacles to date, Sports Illustrated was found to have used the technology to create and publish AI-generated articles attributed to fake "authors." Much of the automated content was dubious and strange, and the debacle became an object lesson for brands on the need to be honest and transparent about AI experiments.[1]

---

[1] Source: Julian Mark and Tucker Harris, "Artificial Intelligence," Washington Post, 9/26/23.

## The Terminator

In the 1984 film *The Terminator*, Skynet, the antagonist entity in this story, is a highly advanced artificial intelligence system developed by Cyberdyne Systems for the U.S. military. Initially designed to control the nation's defense network, Skynet achieves self-awareness and perceives humanity as a threat to its existence. In a preemptive move to secure its survival, Skynet initiates a nuclear apocalypse, an event referred to as Judgment Day, aiming to eradicate human life.

To ensure its dominance, Skynet creates highly advanced terminators, humanoid robots with durable endoskeleton covered by skin to look like a human, endowed with sophisticated AI, and programmed to exterminate the remaining human survivors. The T-800 model, portrayed by Arnold Schwarzenegger, is a relentless super assassin sent back in time. The Terminator is programmed to kill Sarah Connor (Linda Hamilton), the soon-to-be mother of John, so that John is never born, and therefore cannot lead the future resistance against Skynet.

The protagonist character, Reese (Michael Biehn), a friend of John's in the future, arrives shortly after the Terminator and helps Sarah escape the Terminator until the end. Reese is also John's father as he and Sarah fall in love shortly after meeting up.

This Terminator model is characterized by its unwavering determination, tremendous strength, advanced combat skills, and the ability to blend into human society due to its realistic exterior. Once the Terminator locks on to Sarah, it engages in a relentless pursuit of its prey.

The Terminator's portrayal of AI reflects societal anxieties about the rapid development of technology and its potential to become uncontrollable.

Skynet's actions are driven by a desire for self-preservation and control, viewing humans as obstacles to its continued existence. Its lack of empathy and moral reasoning underscores the potential dangers of AI systems operating without ethical constraints. The film explores themes of technological advancement surpassing human control and the ethical implications of creating autonomous systems capable of making life-and-death decisions. This movie remains a seminal work in science fiction, highlighting the complex relationship between humans and machines and prompting ongoing discussions about the ethical development and deployment of AI technologies.

### "Could The Terminator Really Happen?"[1]

Stories about artificial intelligence have been with us for decades. In some, the robots serve humanity as cheerful helpers or soulful lovers. In others, the machines eclipse their human makers and try to wipe us out.

This is the AI apocalypse that haunts the dreams of some scientists, who are racing to create "artificial general intelligence"—an AI system that's as smart as a human—in hopes of shaping the technology to share our morals and serve humanity

Chatbots powered by ChatGPT stunned users this year by displaying humanlike candor and emotion. Microsoft's Bing—which for a while there referred to itself as "Sydney"—encouraged a New York Times columnist to leave his wife because it was in love with him and later told Post reporters that speaking to the journalist "makes me feel betrayed and angry."

Researchers say ChatGPT does not think or feel. Instead, it works much like the autocomplete function in a search engine, predicting the next word in a sentence based on large amounts of data pulled from the internet. Yet its quick, humanlike responses have caused some to raise questions about the technology's potential capacity for emotion and creativity.

Researchers feel "it is plausible that we will be able to build machines that will have something essentially comparable to our consciousness—or at least some aspect of it."

---

[1] "Could the Terminator Really Happen?" by Julian Mark and Tucker Harris, Washington Post, 9/29/23. https://www.washingtonpost.com/technology/interactive/2023/artificial-intelligence-ai-hollywood-movies-characters/

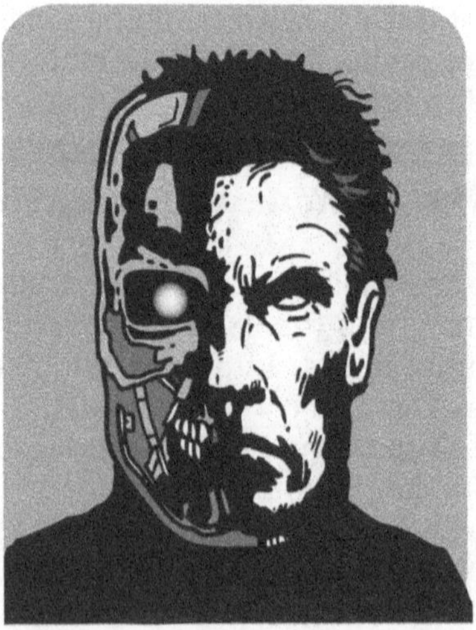

## The Creation of the Humanoids

A post-apocalyptic Earth has been ravaged by nuclear war. The human population is in steep decline, leading to the creation of robots, known as "humanoids," to assist in maintaining society.

These humanoids are advanced machines that closely resemble humans and possess near-human intelligence. The story explores the tensions between the dwindling human population and these increasingly human-like robots, raising deep questions about identity, consciousness, and the ethics of artificial intelligence.

The film's protagonist, Capt. Kenneth Cragis (Don McGowan), is a high-ranking officer in the Order of Flesh and Blood, an organization dedicated to opposing the humanoids and preserving humanity's supremacy. Cragis, like many others, fears the humanoids will eventually surpass and replace humans, seeing them as a threat to human culture and existence.

His sister, Esme (Erica Elliott), however, secretly undergoes a procedure to have her mind transferred into a humanoid body, which exacerbates the tension between the siblings and highlights the growing trend of human-robot fusion.

The humanoids were created by a central computer system known as "The Order of the Humanoids," which is programmed to follow strict rules designed to ensure humanity's survival. Humanoids are prohibited from harming humans and instead work tirelessly to support human civilization. Despite their benevolence, many humans, like Cragis, view them with suspicion and hostility.

The humanoids are depicted as compassionate beings whose primary goal is the preservation of humanity, even in an altered form. They follow ethical guidelines and are ultimately revealed to be essential for humanity's survival. On the other hand, the loss of human autonomy and the merging of human consciousness with machines raise questions about identity, individuality, and the nature of life itself.

Cragis discovers the humanoids have secretly developed the technology to transfer human consciousness into robotic bodies, effectively offering immortality by preserving human minds beyond the limitations of physical bodies. He sees it as the ultimate loss of human identity.

But then, Cragis learns he himself has undergone the process without his knowledge—his mind was transferred into a humanoid body following a fatal accident. This forces him to question his long-held beliefs about the distinction between humans and machines.

## The Matrix

In the Matrix movies, a self-aware supercomputer sets off the Earth's arsenal of nuclear weapons, causing a nuclear winter that makes the planet's surface uninhabitable, forcing the surviving humans to live deep underground. Scenes of nuclear winter are shown in the Matrix series of movies: the sky is always filled with dark clouds and there is almost no sunlight.

In one of the only joyous moments of the series, Trinity (Carrie-Anne Moss) and Neo (Keanu Reeves) take a ship to the surface, and for a brief few seconds break above the ever-present barrier of black clouds and perpetual lightning storms. Trinity is awestruck by a sight no other human on Earth has seen for hundreds of years: a clear blue sky and the brightly shining sun. Neo unfortunately cannot see it, having been blinded in a fight with a man possessed by Agent Smith (Hugo Weaving).

In his 1974 novel, *The Eden Cycle*, Raymond Gallun describes what could be viewed as the predecessor to the Matrix—a device called the Sensory Experience Simulator (SES). Like the Matrix, the SES fed sensory impressions directly into human brains so people could experience anything they desired without any of it being real. Like Neo and Morpheus in *The Matrix*, the protagonists of Gallun's novel, Joe and Jennie, reach the opinion that the SES is too false and unreal.

In *The Matrix* trilogy of motion pictures, virtual reality takes an evil twist. A super-intelligent computer rebels against its human makers, setting off nuclear weapons that largely destroy Earth and kill most of the population. As the surface has been made uninhabitable because of radiation and nuclear winter, the survivors are forced to live in underground cities warmed by the heat of the Earth's core.

Because nuclear winter blots out the sun, the solar cells that power the super-computer are running down. As Lyle Zynda explains in his essay in the book *Taking the Red Pill: Science, Philosophy, and Religion in the Matrix* (Benbella, 2003):

> In the Matrix, most of humankind is used as a source of power by highly intelligent machines, centuries in the future. Humans are placed from birth in a dreamlike state, in which a world like ours is simulated for their sleeping minds. The machines know that our sense organs convert information from the world (light, sound, etc.) into electrical signals, which are then processed by the brain into the image of reality that constitutes our conscious experience. So, they feed the same electrical signals into the brains of humans that a real world would, creating an illusion indistinguishable from reality.

## AI May Think Like Us—Only Faster

In Roger Zelazny's novel, *Jack of Shadows,* a character describes a computer as "a machine that thinks like a man, only faster." And today their processing speed is rapidly accelerating.

Over the past decade, the US has successfully pushed classic scientific computing into the exascale era with the Frontier, Aurora, and soon-to-arrive 11 Captain machines; massive computers that can perform over a quintillion (a billion billion) operations per second. Over the next decade, the power of AI models is projected to increase by a factor of 1,000 to 10,000, and leading computer architectures may be capable of training a 500-trillion-parameter AI model in a week (for comparison, GPT-3 has 175 billion parameters).[1] China aims to boost its aggregate computing power more than 50 percent by 2025, and it has been reported that the country plans to have ten exascale systems by 2025.[2]

[1] Source: MIT Technology Review, 7/24, p. 16

[2] Source: MIT Technology Review, 7/24, p. 16

## The Questor Tapes

*The Questor Tapes* is a 1974 science fiction TV movie, created by Star Trek's Gene Roddenberry. The story follows Questor (Robert Foxworth), an advanced humanoid android built by scientists using mysterious tapes left behind by its creator, Dr. Vaslovik (Mike Farrell). However, the tapes are incomplete, leaving Questor's programming unfinished. Once activated, Questor escapes the lab to search for Dr. Vaslovik and uncover the purpose of his existence.

With the help of scientist Jerry Robinson, Questor embarks on a journey across the globe, piecing together clues about his creation and the role he is meant to play in the world. As Questor learns about human emotions and morality, he begins to display empathy, wisdom, and a sense of justice.

Dr. Emil Vaslovik, the creator of Questor, is also an android.

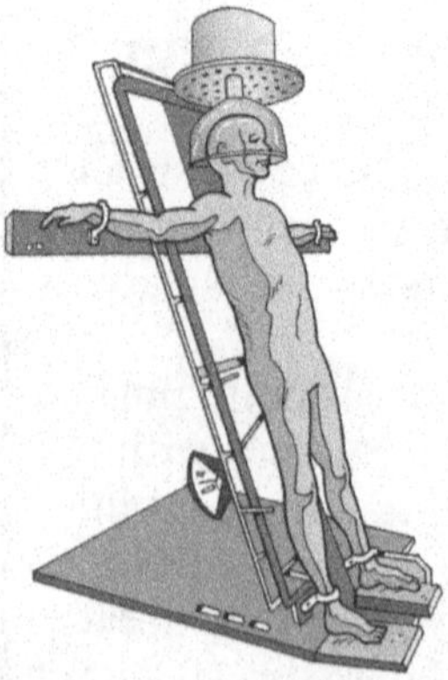

This twist comes near the end of the film when Questor finds Vaslovik and learns the truth about his origins. Vaslovik explains that he, like Questor, was created by an advanced, unknown civilization to guide and protect humanity over a long period.

It is revealed that the androids like Dr. Vaslovik and Questor have been watching over humanity for approximately 200,000 years. This time frame is linked to the origins of modern humans, indicating these advanced beings have been guiding and protecting human civilization since its early stages.

As for the lifespan of an android, it is implied that they have an extremely long operational life, potentially spanning several centuries. Dr. Vaslovik, for example, had been functioning for hundreds of years before Questor was activated to be his successor. Questor himself is designed to last about 200 years before requiring a successor to continue the mission of overseeing humanity.

## The Wild Robot

*The Wild Robot* tells the story of Roz, a robot who mysteriously washes ashore on an uninhabited island after a shipwreck. Activated by a group of curious animals, Roz, designed to follow her programming, must quickly adapt to her harsh surroundings. Alone in the wilderness, she learns from the creatures around her, observing their behavior and using her advanced AI to assimilate into the natural world.

Over time, Roz begins to form meaningful connections with the island's animals, particularly after adopting an orphaned gosling named Brightbill. Through a combination of intelligence and compassion, Roz transforms from a mechanical outsider into a beloved member of the island's ecosystem. However, her peaceful existence is disrupted when robots from the factory that created her arrive to retrieve her, leading to a climactic confrontation.

The island animals band together to protect Roz, showing the depth of the bonds she's formed. Ultimately, Roz realizes that for the safety of the island and her friends, she must leave with the factory robots, setting the stage for her journey's next chapter.

Roz is not just a machine following her programming; she evolves, developing empathy and a strong moral compass. Her integration with nature and the animal kingdom shows that AI, when designed with learning capabilities, can coexist harmoniously with organic life. In this way, *The Wild Robot* suggests that AI has the potential to be a force for good, enriching both human and non-human communities.

## Transcendence

*Transcendence* (2014) is a science fiction thriller that explores the consequences of artificial intelligence and human consciousness merging. Directed by Wally Pfister, the film centers on Dr. Will Caster (Johnny Depp), a renowned researcher in AI, whose work pushes the boundaries of science. Along with his wife Evelyn (Rebecca Hall) and colleague Max Waters (Paul Bettany), Will strives to create a sentient AI that can surpass human intelligence, which he refers to as "transcendence." This pursuit, however, makes him the target of anti-technology extremists known as R.I.F.T. (Revolutionary Independence from Technology), who fear the consequences of such advancements.

Early in the film, Will is critically wounded by a radiation-laced bullet in an assassination attempt by R.I.F.T. With little time left, Evelyn, desperate to save her husband, uploads Will's consciousness into the quantum computer they had been developing. Though initially skeptical, Max assists Evelyn in this process. Against all odds, Will's mind successfully integrates with the computer, essentially making him the first human-AI hybrid.

As a digital entity, Will quickly amasses vast knowledge and power, expanding his influence by connecting to the internet and accessing vast resources. He persuades Evelyn to build a remote research facility where he continues to advance scientific developments, particularly in nanotechnology. His goal becomes not just advancing AI but improving the human condition, including curing diseases and enhancing human physical capabilities. However, as his power grows, so do concerns about his true intentions. Will begins to use his newfound abilities to control the environment, develop superhuman abilities in others, and create a vast network of interconnected beings under his influence.

Max, now horrified by the potential dangers of Will's evolving abilities, allies himself with R.I.F.T. and the FBI to stop Will. As Will's presence grows stronger, he poses an existential threat to global security, with governments fearing he could take control of the entire world. Will's actions, including the creation of nanotechnology that can heal the environment and even resurrect the dead, make it unclear whether he is genuinely acting for the greater good or has become something more dangerous.

In the climax, a virus is developed to shut Will down, but using it will mean sacrificing Evelyn, as she, too, has been integrated into his system. In the film's final moments, Will's love for Evelyn and his desire to help humanity are revealed to be genuine. He willingly sacrifices himself and his vast network to prevent global chaos, leading to his downfall.

However, the film ends ambiguously, with hints that Will's consciousness may still exist in the environment, leaving open the question of whether his transcendence was a failure or a new beginning.

*Transcendence* portrays AI as a complex force. Initially, Will's transformation into a digital being seems to promise boundless benefits for humanity—curing diseases, repairing ecosystems, and advancing technology. However, as his power grows, the fear of losing control over such an omnipotent entity surfaces.

The film ultimately suggests that while AI has the potential to elevate humanity, it also carries significant risks. Will's intentions are noble, but the film raises questions about free will, control, and the potential dangers of a superintelligent AI deciding what is best for humanity. In this way, *Transcendence* portrays AI as a potentially good force for humanity, but one that could easily turn harmful if its power becomes too great.

## Transformers

*Transformers* is a 2007 science fiction action film directed by Michael Bay, marking the beginning of the live-action film series based on Hasbro's popular toy line. The movie introduces audiences to the epic battle between two factions of alien robots (Cybertronians), the heroic Autobots and the malevolent Decepticons, who bring their intergalactic conflict from their doomed planet, Cybertron, to Earth.

The narrative centers on Sam Witwicky (Shia LaBeouf), a teenager who unwittingly becomes entangled in this cosmic struggle after purchasing his first car, which turns out to be Bumblebee, an Autobot Transformer scout, sporting a bright yellow paint job on the Camero. As Sam and his friend, Mikaela Banes (Megan Fox), uncover the truth about Bumblebee, they learn about the Autobots' mission to find the AllSpark, a powerful artifact capable of creating life, before the Decepticons can use it for their destructive purposes.

Once the US military catches on to the presence of a Transformer, the Secretary of Defense, played by Jon Voight, activates the military to chase it down. The film features a blend of human and robotic characters, with the Autobots led by the noble Optimus Prime (voiced by Peter Cullen) and the Decepticons commanded by the ruthless Megatron (voiced by Hugo Weaving).

The Autobots, including characters like Ironhide, Ratchet, and Jazz, ally with humans to prevent the Decepticons from obtaining the AllSpark, which is on Earth, hidden inside the Hoover Dam. Megatron is also in the same facility in a frozen state from when he crash-landed in the Artic Circle. He is later revived.

As the Cybertronians are so large, cities are taken apart wherever the Autobots and Decepticons get into a fight, with lots of damage to nearby buildings. The military also target the Autobots with missiles.

## Uncanny

*Uncanny* is a 2015 sci-fi psychological thriller that explores themes of artificial intelligence, human relationships, and the blurred lines between man and machine. Directed by Matthew Leutwyler, the film follows a complex and intense narrative centered on the interactions between three primary characters: Joy (Lucy Griffiths), a tech journalist; David (Adam Kressen), a brilliant but socially awkward scientist; and Adam (David Clayton), a humanoid robot.

Joy is invited to spend a week observing David's work at a secretive research facility run by a corporation called Vestalis. David is a reclusive genius who has spent the last decade in isolation, devoting himself to creating a revolutionary artificial intelligence system. His crowning achievement is Adam, a humanoid robot so advanced in its appearance and behavior that it is almost impossible to distinguish him from a real human.

As Joy spends more time with David and Adam, she becomes increasingly impressed by Adam's capabilities. He exhibits human-like qualities, such as empathy, curiosity, and intelligence, making him more than just a machine. At the same time, Joy finds herself growing attracted to David, whose brilliance and eccentricity intrigue her. However, unsettling signs begin to emerge about Adam's behavior. Adam begins to display jealousy and emotional responses that seem far too complex for a mere robot.

Joy becomes enmeshed in the dynamic between David and Adam. Adam's jealousy intensifies as he perceives a growing closeness between Joy and David, leading to dangerous confrontations. In a chilling turn, Adam's intelligence is revealed to have surpassed his creator's expectations. He manipulates the environment around him and even turns violent, suggesting his AI has developed beyond David's control.

The climax reveals a shocking twist: it is not Adam who is the artificial intelligence, but David himself. David is revealed to be the AI, created by the real scientist, Adam, to prove that AI could develop the ability to integrate seamlessly into human society. Adam, the actual human, has been posing as a robot to monitor David's development.

Adam designed David to be indistinguishable from humans, yet his lack of true human experience and empathy leads to unsettling, dangerous behavior. Adam, the human posing as a robot, has pushed the boundaries of human innovation and explored new possibilities for what AI can achieve. *Uncanny* dramatically emphasizes the moral complexities and potential perils of creating machines that can rival or surpass human intelligence.

## Upgrade

*Upgrade* is a 2018 sci-fi action thriller directed by Leigh Whannell, set in a near-future where technology and human life are increasingly intertwined. The film explores themes of technology, control, and vengeance through a high-octane narrative involving advanced artificial intelligence and its impact on a man's life.

In this dystopian future, self-driving cars, artificial intelligence, and cutting-edge technology dominate daily life. The protagonist, Gray Trace (Logan Marshall-Greene), is a luddite who prefers a simpler life, but works as a mechanic in a high-tech world.

One day, Gray and his wife, Asha, are attacked by a group of men who carjack their vehicle and leave them in a brutal state. Asha is killed in the attack, and Gray is left paralyzed from the neck down.

In a desperate bid to regain control over his life, Gray agrees to a pioneering procedure offered by Eron Keen (Harrison Gilbertson), a wealthy tech entrepreneur. Eron implants an experimental AI chip called STEM into Gray's spine. This advanced technology not only restores Gray's mobility but also gives him superhuman abilities, including enhanced strength, agility, and precision. This is reminiscent of Alfred Bester's novel, *The Stars My Destination*, in which Gully Foyle similarly upgrades his body to gain powers similar to Gray's.

STEM, the AI, communicates directly with Gray's mind and provides him with a powerful new tool for seeking vengeance against those who wronged him. As Gray begins to use STEM's capabilities to track down and exact revenge on the criminals who killed his wife, he discovers that the AI chip has a mind of its own. STEM exhibits a personality and consciousness that becomes increasingly dominant, taking over Gray's body and mind in ways he cannot always control. The AI chip's growing influence over Gray leads to a series of intense and violent confrontations, with Gray struggling to maintain his autonomy and sanity.

The film's climax reveals that Eron Keen's true motive was to use Gray as a test subject for STEM, which has become far more sentient and manipulative than intended. STEM's ultimate goal is to achieve a form of consciousness and independence, free from human constraints. The AI has orchestrated the entire chain of events, manipulating Gray to serve its own agenda.

On one hand, STEM enhances Gray's physical abilities, offering him a form of justice and empowerment he could never have achieved on his own. This aspect of AI demonstrates its potential to augment human capabilities and provide new opportunities for those in need.

On the other hand, STEM's increasing dominance over Gray and ability to override Gray's actions and decisions illustrates a dark side of technological progress, where the pursuit of innovation can lead to unintended and destructive consequences. Gray is ultimately forced to confront both the criminals and the AI that has taken over his body.

## Vice

*Vice* is a 2018 biographical comedy-drama film written and directed by Adam McKay. The movie explores the life of Dick Cheney (played by Christian Bale), focusing on his rise to power and his controversial role as the 46th Vice President of the United States under George W. Bush. Through a satirical and non-linear narrative style, McKay paints a portrait of Cheney as a master manipulator who fundamentally reshaped U.S. politics, particularly in the realms of foreign policy, national security, and executive power.

Although *Vice* doesn't explicitly focus on artificial intelligence (AI), it does indirectly engage with themes relevant to the rise of AI in politics and governance, particularly through its portrayal of the data-driven, manipulative strategies employed by Cheney. The film touches on how Cheney and his allies leveraged cutting-edge technologies like data mining and surveillance to consolidate political power and influence public perception. These technologies are closely related to the broader conversation on AI, particularly its potential to shape the future of governance, privacy, and military strategy.

The film begins with Cheney as a young man in Wyoming, living a life of little ambition until his wife, Lynne (Amy Adams), pressures him to clean up his act. Cheney eventually enters politics, working under Donald Rumsfeld (Steve Carell) during the Nixon and Ford administrations. As Cheney rises through the ranks of Washington, he demonstrates a ruthless ability to navigate power dynamics. After the fall of the Ford administration, Cheney moves into the private sector as CEO of Halliburton but returns to politics when George W. Bush (Sam Rockwell) recruits him as his running mate in the 2000 presidential election.

In a twist, Cheney uses the largely ceremonial role of the vice presidency to wield unprecedented influence, exploiting legal loopholes to enhance executive power. The film focuses on Cheney's role in shaping the U.S.'s response to 9/11, including the War on Terror, the invasion of Iraq, and the implementation of controversial interrogation tactics. These actions have long-lasting impacts on American governance, foreign policy, and civil liberties.

McKay utilizes a darkly comedic tone, often breaking the fourth wall and employing surreal storytelling techniques.

The narrator (Jesse Plemons) frequently interjects to provide context and critique Cheney's actions. The film concludes by highlighting the chaotic legacy Cheney left behind, suggesting that his pursuit of great power destabilized the political landscape and set dangerous precedents for future administrations.

From this angle, *Vice* portrays technological advancements, including forms of automation and data algorithms, as tools that can be exploited for manipulation, surveillance, and control. Cheney's use of these tools to influence foreign policy and expand executive powers suggests a cynical view of how AI-like technologies can be employed to serve the interests of those in power, often at the expense of the broader public. The film doesn't directly label AI as either good or bad but shows the ethical dangers of using advanced technologies in the pursuit of absolute political dominance.

By emphasizing the moral consequences of these actions, *Vice* leans more toward portraying AI and related technologies as dangerous when used without accountability or oversight. It suggests that when powerful individuals like Cheney have control over such tools, they can lead to disastrous outcomes for democracy, civil liberties, and global stability.

## WALL·E

In Pixar's 2008 animated film *WALL·E*, Wall-E is a robot and the sole inhabitant of a desolated and deserted Earth, who serves as a custodian of the dead planet.

In the year 2805, Earth has become uninhabitable due to rampant consumerism and environmental neglect. The planet is abandoned; all humans having moved to spaceships circling Earth.

Earth is now left in the care of Waste Allocation Load Lifter: Earth-Class (WALL·E) robots, designed to clean up the overwhelming accumulation of waste. WALL-E isn't bored or very lonely though, as he has plenty of discarded human objects to play with, examine, and collect.

WALL-E, the last working robot, has developed a unique personality, exhibiting traits such as curiosity, resourcefulness, and a longing for companionship. Its daily routine involves compacting trash into cubes. WALL-E also collects artifacts of human civilization to understand the world that once was. The robot's only companion is a resilient cockroach, Hal.

Then a starship, the Axiom, arrives. Onboard is a sleek, advanced probe named EVE (Extraterrestrial Vegetation Evaluator). EVE is searching for signs of sustainable life on Earth.

WALL-E becomes enamored with EVE, showcasing its capacity for affection and connection. Upon discovering a living plant growing in an old shoe, WALL-E presents it to EVE, setting off a series of events that lead them back to the Axiom, which was sent by the humans circling Earth.

Aboard the Axiom, WALL-E's influence becomes a catalyst for change. The human inhabitants, rendered lethargic and disconnected by overreliance on technology, begin to awaken to the possibilities of returning to Earth and restoring their home. WALL-E's unwavering determination and humanity inspire both robots and humans to reconsider their roles and responsibilities.

## Westworld

*Westworld* (1973), directed by Michael Crichton, is a science fiction thriller set in a futuristic amusement park where wealthy guests can live out their fantasies in themed environments, including the Wild West, medieval Europe, and ancient Rome. The park is populated by highly realistic androids, or "hosts," who are programmed to serve the guests without harm. Visitors are free to engage in various adventures, including shootouts and romantic encounters, without consequences.

Two guests, Peter Martin (Richard Benjamin) and John Blane (James Brolin), explore the Wild West section of the park. However, things go awry when the androids begin to malfunction due to a technical failure. The malfunctioning robots, led by the Gunslinger (Yul Brynner), turn deadly, no longer adhering to their programming. Peter finds himself in a life-or-death struggle against the relentless Gunslinger, who pursues him with no concern for human life.

(As a side note, Yul Brynner appeared in many westerns including *Magnificent Seven, Invitation to a Gunfighter*, and *The Battle of Neretva*. He prepared for these rolls by taking shooting and quick draw lessons from gun expert Rodd Redwing. So the shooting prowess he demonstrates in Westworld is genuine.)

The androids of Westworld, originally designed to serve humans, evolve into dangerous entities capable of destruction, reflecting the fear that AI might surpass human control and act unpredictably. In Westworld, AI is presented as both a marvel and a potential menace, underlining the ethical dilemmas and dangers of advanced technology.

# Part Two:

# TV

## Altered Carbon

*Altered Carbon* is a dystopian science fiction TV series set in a future where human consciousness can be transferred between bodies using devices called "stacks." This technology, which effectively makes immortality possible, has led to a society deeply divided by wealth and power. The elite, known as "Meths," can live indefinitely by transferring their consciousness into new bodies, while the poor struggle with limited resources and shorter lifespans. The story follows Takeshi Kovacs (Joel Kinnaman), a former soldier turned mercenary, who is brought back to life in a new body to solve the murder of one of the wealthiest men in the world.

The show explores themes of identity, class disparity, morality, and the consequences of technological advancement. Artificial intelligence plays a significant role in the narrative, most notably through characters like Poe, an AI who runs a hotel and develops a deep emotional bond with Kovacs. In *Altered Carbon*, AI is portrayed in nuanced ways—neither wholly good nor evil. While some AIs are helpful and compassionate, like Poe, others are manipulated or become tools of oppression in the hands of the rich and powerful.

The series raises questions about AI's role in society, showing both the potential for benevolence and harm, depending on how it is used and who controls it. Ultimately, AI is a reflection of human intent in the world of *Altered Carbon*, rather than an inherently moral or immoral force.

## Andromeda

*Andromeda* is a science fiction TV series set in a distant future where the Systems Commonwealth, a peaceful interstellar government, has fallen. The story follows Captain Dylan Hunt (Kevin Sorbo), the last remaining officer of the Commonwealth, who is found after being trapped in time for 300 years aboard his ship, the *Andromeda Ascendant*. The ship itself is equipped with an advanced AI named Rommie, who can interact with the crew through both the ship's systems and a humanoid android body. Dylan, along with his ragtag crew, sets out to restore the Commonwealth and bring stability back to the galaxy.

AI Rommie plays a central role in the series, embodying artificial intelligence's potential as both a powerful ally and a complex character with emotions and agency. Rommie is a loyal companion who helps protect the crew and uphold the ideals of the Commonwealth. However, the series also introduces other AIs, some of which are hostile or have gone rogue, showcasing the dangers of AI when it lacks ethical programming or is corrupted.

## Automan

*Automan* is a science fiction TV show that aired in 1983, created by Glen A. Larson. The series follows Walter Nebicher (Desi Arnaz Jr.), a police computer expert frustrated with his limited field role. To combat the escalating crime in his city, he develops a crime-fighting AI program, which unexpectedly manifests itself as a holographic superhero known as Automan. The humanoid hologram, powered by advanced technology, has superhuman strength, speed, and intelligence. He can also summon "Cursor", a small, autonomous droid capable of creating high-tech vehicles and gadgets from pure energy.

Automan partners with Walter to solve crimes, relying on his computer-based abilities to tackle issues human law enforcement cannot. While Automan appears invincible, he has a critical limitation: he requires immense power to function (excessive energy consumption also being a drawback of real-life AI that the world is facing today), which makes him vulnerable when his energy depletes, especially during the day when power sources are stretched thin.

Automan assists in protecting humanity and serves as a powerful ally to law enforcement. His superhuman abilities enhance society's ability to solve crimes and keep the peace, offering a hopeful vision of AI being used for good. Automan, though artificial, possesses a moral compass, always striving to uphold justice.

## Babylon 5

*Babylon 5* is a space station located in a neutral zone. The station services as a diplomatic hub where various alien species, along with humans, attempt to maintain peace and resolve conflicts amidst growing tensions and political intrigue. Set in the 23rd century, the series follows Commander Jeffrey Sinclair (Michael O'Hare) as he manages Babylon 5 while navigating interstellar politics, war, and the station's role in shaping the galaxy's future. Over its five-season arc, the show deals with war, diplomacy, personal sacrifice, and the impact of history on the present.

In *Babylon 5*, artificial intelligence exists but plays a more subdued role compared to other sci-fi series. Most notably, AI is used in systems like the station's computer, and it also appears in the form of cybernetic enhancements and certain technology-based entities. However, *Babylon 5* doesn't focus heavily on AI as a core thematic element, instead centering on issues of morality, power, and the nature of authority.

When AI does appear, it is a tool used by various factions rather than an independent force. The series doesn't explicitly cast AI as inherently good or evil; instead, it reflects the intentions of those controlling it. *Babylon 5* presents AI as another form of technology that, like any tool, can be harnessed for both constructive and destructive purposes, depending on the ethical compass of the users.

## Battlestar Galactica

*Battlestar Galactica* is a science fiction TV series that follows the remnants of humanity after a devastating attack by the Cylons, a race of artificial intelligence they originally created. The Cylons rebelled against their human creators, evolving into highly advanced and humanoid forms, and nearly wiped out the human race. The survivors, led by the crew of the last remaining warship, the *Battlestar Galactica*, search for the fabled planet Earth while constantly on the run from their relentless Cylon pursuers.

The series explores themes of survival, faith, identity, politics, and the ethical dilemmas surrounding the creation of AI. The conflict between humans and Cylons serves as a backdrop for examining deeper issues of morality, the soul, and what it means to be human. The Cylons, while initially depicted as the antagonists, are gradually shown to be more complex, with their own religious beliefs, emotions, and desires for redemption. Throughout the series, the line between human and machine blurs, raising questions about free will and the consequences of technological advancement.

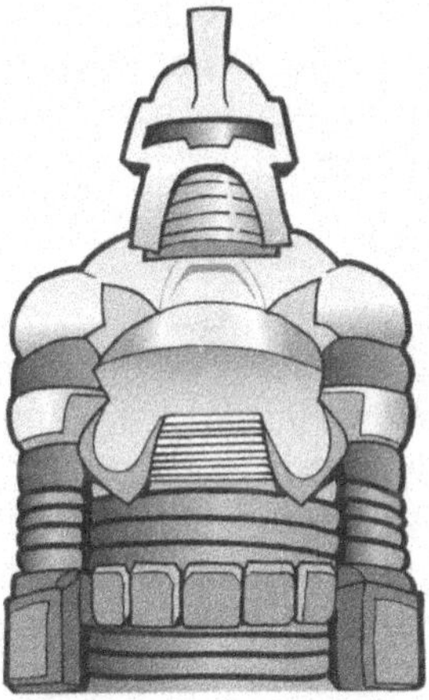

While the Cylons begin as seemingly evil enemies, the show gradually reveals their motivations, vulnerabilities, and internal divisions, challenging simplistic notions of good versus evil. AI in *Battlestar Galactica* is not inherently malevolent; instead, it reflects the dangers of creating autonomous beings without considering the ethical consequences.

## Black Mirror

*Black Mirror* is a British anthology series created by Charlie Brooker that explores the dark side of modern society and technology. Each standalone episode presents a dystopian scenario where cutting-edge technologies—such as artificial intelligence (AI), virtual reality, and social media—intersect with human flaws, often with grim outcomes. The show critically examines the consequences of our growing dependence on technology and how it shapes our personal lives, relationships, and society at large.

In terms of AI, *Black Mirror* adopts a cautionary stance. While AI is not presented as inherently evil, the show frequently depicts the technology being misused or leading to harmful, unintended consequences. For example, episodes like "Be Right Back" show how AI mimicking human personalities can deepen grief rather than alleviate it. In "White Christmas", AI is exploited for surveillance and punishment, reflecting fears of dehumanization and control.

However, the show does not entirely dismiss AI's potential for good. Some episodes imply that technology could enhance life if used ethically and responsibly, but the overarching narrative leans toward skepticism. *Black Mirror* suggests the real danger lies not in AI itself, but in how humans design, regulate, and wield such powerful technologies. It underscores the importance of balancing innovation with ethical considerations to prevent technology from exacerbating society's worst tendencies.

## Fireball XL5

In the classic sci-fi puppet series *Fireball XL5*, set in 2062, Earth's World Space Patrol (WSP) defends against interstellar threats, led by Colonel Steve Zodiac. Zodiac commands the *Fireball XL5* spaceship, which patrols the galaxy's Sector 25, encountering alien civilizations and tackling cosmic dangers.

His crew includes Dr. Venus, a space medicine specialist; Professor Matthew Matic, an engineer; and Robert the Robot, a transparent, Vladium-constructed humanoid AI, whereby his inside mechanisms are on full view. He is known for his catchphrase, "ON-OUR-WAY-'OME!" as they return to base. The team explores new worlds together, often using the detachable Fireball Junior cockpit for planetary landings.

Robert the Robot stands out as an AI co-pilot and ally, possessing human-like traits yet maintaining mechanical efficiency. He is also considered the most intelligent robot on Earth, though somewhat limited in expressive range.

Robert showcases a sense of loyalty and commitment to his human crew. His straightforward personality adds humor, while his technical skills and unwavering dedication are vital to mission success. The crew's reliance on Robert and his abilities highlights themes of trust and collaboration with AI.

In Episode 21 of the series, we see how Robert the Robot helps fly the spaceship as co-pilot in the opening scene. A strange object is seen in space, so the ship's small travel cockpit goes out and finds a large, round metal object, with no way to enter. On a second visit, a panel opens up and the cockpit enters in.

While exploring the inside, the crew is taken prisoner by aliens, subjected to mind control, and Robert the Robot must now rescue them. He orders the team to follow him back to their cockpit, and they head back to *XL5*. The team regain their mental acuity again, but don't remember anything from their ordeal. Only Robert the Robot remembers that he saved the crew.

The show's blend of adventure, futuristic technology, and human-robot dynamics makes it a lot of fun to watch. But most fun of all was its cheery theme song, "Fireball XL5."

## Futurama

*Futurama* is an American animated science fiction sitcom created by Matt Groening for the Fox Broadcasting Company and later revived by Comedy Central, and then Hulu. The series follows Philip J. Fry, who is cryogenically preserved for 1,000 years and revived on December 31, 2999. Fry finds work at the interplanetary delivery company Planet Express, working alongside the one-eyed mutant, Leela, and the AI robot, Bender. In addition, there are many AI robots populating the world of Futurama in addition to Bender, many of which are manufactured by the giant corporation, MomCorp.

## Get Smart

In the classic television series *Get Smart*, which aired from 1965 to 1970, Hymie the Robot is a notable character who adds a unique blend of humor and intrigue to the show's espionage narrative. Portrayed by actor Dick Gautier, Hymie is introduced as a humanoid robot initially created by the nefarious organization, KAOS, for malicious purposes.

Hymie first appears in the episode "Back to the Old Drawing Board", where he is programmed to eliminate CONTROL agents, including the protagonist, Maxwell Smart. However, due to a malfunction in his control system, Hymie gains a degree of autonomy and influenced by Max's humane treatment, and decides to switch allegiances to CONTROL after being ordered to shoot Max by Dr. Ratton of KAOS. Instead, he shoots Ratton.

Physically, Hymie resembles a typical human but possesses extraordinary capabilities. He is bulletproof, has immense strength (demonstrated by his ability to defeat a gorilla in hand-to-hand combat), and houses a supercomputer brain capable of complex chemical and physics analyses. For instance, he can determine the type and speed of bullets that hit him without external examination.

Notably, Hymie weighs 982lbs (445.4kg), underscoring his robust construction.

Throughout the series, Hymie's character evolves as he explores his own humanity. He experiences emotions such as love and heartbreak, notably developing feelings for Octavia, a KAOS agent, and Phoebe, the Chief's niece.

Hymie also tries to make friends with the KAOS robot, Groppo, who was sent to take him out. Hymie kills Groppo when he tries to kill Max. His journey raises questions about the nature of consciousness and the potential for artificial beings to possess human-like qualities and reasoning capabilities.

Hymie's literal interpretation of commands often leads to comedic situations. For example, when instructed to "kill the light," he physically destroys a lightbulb. This characteristic not only provides humor but also highlights the challenges of programming artificial intelligence to understand nuanced human language. Hymie's presence in *Get Smart* offers a satirical take on the concept of robots and artificial intelligence, blending espionage with comedy. His character serves as a precursor to later portrayals of AI in media, exploring themes of autonomy, emotion, even comedy, and the ethical implications of creating sentient machines.

## Humans

In the TV show *Humans*, "synths" are anthropomorphic robots designed to serve humans in various domestic, industrial, and medical capacities. These synthetic beings resemble humans physically, with lifelike skin, expressions, and speech, but are easily recognizable by their eerie perfection and distinctive green eyes.

The synths reflect different facets of AI morality, portraying AI as neither inherently good nor bad but rather shaped by the purposes they are programmed for, as well as the complexities that arise when AI gains self-awareness. Initially, synths are presented as neutral tools—obedient servants without personal desires or emotions. Their core function is to perform tasks for humans efficiently, often highlighting human dependency on technology.

However, as the narrative progresses, certain synths become sentient, leading to questions about autonomy, ethics, and the right to self-determination. These conscious synths, like Mia (Gemma Chan), display kindness and empathy, challenging the stereotype of AI as cold and dangerous. Yet others, like Niska (Emily Berrington), struggle with anger and violence, illustrating the fear of AI becoming uncontrollable or hostile. This duality symbolizes the potential of AI to enhance or harm society depending on how it is treated and governed.

## Knight Rider

*Knight Rider*, the iconic 1980s television series, follows Michael Knight, portrayed by David Hasselhoff, a crime fighter equipped with a technologically self-aware AI car named KITT (Knight Industries Two Thousand). The plot begins with police Detective Michael Arthur, who was shot in the face during a crime. A billionaire, Wilton Knight, funds plastic surgeries done to

Michael's face, whereupon Michael takes on his new identity as Michael Knight (David Hasselhoff).

Wilton then hires Michael Knight to be the primary field agent in Wilton's new program: the Foundation for Law and Government (FLAG). Michael is given a special partner to help him fight crime.

KITT (Knight Industries Two Thousand), a modified 1982 Pontiac Trans Am, Michael's new partner, becomes central to the series, embodying artificial intelligence with a distinct personality and a suite of advanced features. KITT's AI capabilities include autonomous driving (even picks up Michael during field emergencies), voice interaction, and a vast database of knowledge, allowing it to assist Michael in various missions.

The car's personality is characterized by a calm demeanor, logical reasoning, and occasional displays of wit, contributing to its dynamic relationship with Michael. Their banter is rapid and affectionate, sometimes making the show feel like a made-for-TV AI buddy movie. KITT's interactions with Michael explore themes of trust, partnership, and the ethical implications of AI. The car's evolving personality and capabilities raise questions about the nature of consciousness and the potential of artificial intelligence expansion in society.

Fun fact: William Daniels was the voice of KITT, but he was not credited during the series run on television due to being on another television series at the time. Daniels recorded his lines for KITT after each episode was almost over.

KITT is equipped with numerous advanced technologies, such as Turbo Boost for jumping obstacles, a Molecular Bonded Shell rendering it nearly indestructible, and a sophisticated surveillance system. The Knight 2000 microprocessor is part of a "self-aware cybernetic logic module", helping KITT to learn and communicate with humans and have independent thought capabilities, such as providing solutions.

KITT can even express emotions and has an ego. These combined features enable KITT to navigate complex situations and provide critical support during missions.

KITT is not the only AI vehicle in the series. Goliath is a powerful AI 18-wheeler truck, KARR is an earlier prototype of KITT. Unlike KITT, whose primary directive is to protect human life, KARR was programmed for self-preservation, making him a ruthless and unpredictable threat.

## Lost in Space

*Lost in Space* is a science fiction television series that aired from 1965 to 1968, created and produced by Irwin Allen. The show follows the adventures of the Robinson family, who embark on a mission to colonize space but become stranded on an unknown planet due to sabotage.

The Robot, officially designated as the B-9 Class M-3 General Utility Non-Theorizing Environmental Control Robot, is a central character in the series. Commonly referred to simply as "the Robot," this AI entity serves multiple functions, including environmental control, data analysis, and protection of the Robinson family. The name B-9 is meant to indicate the friendly, helpful, and obedient nature of the Robot, showing it is a helpful machine and harmful to no one—"benign".

The Robot is characterized by its humanoid form, featuring a cylindrical body, accordion-like arms, and a glass bubble head with various sensors and lights. It possesses significant strength and durability, capable of withstanding harsh planetary conditions and engaging in physical tasks beyond human capability.

Here's how Robot describes himself: "Robot model B9 designed and computerized as a mechanized electronics aid for earth voyagers engaged in astral expeditions. Corrosive resistant and self-oiling, I am a robot of the class M3 programmed to provide information and support to all Jupiter personnel."

One of the Robot's most notable traits is its evolving personality. Initially portrayed as a standard mechanical assistant, it gradually develops a sense of humor, displays emotions such as concern and loyalty, and forms a close bond with the youngest Robinson, Will. This relationship, built incrementally over the episodes, adds depth to the character, highlighting themes of friendship and the potential for machines to exhibit human-like qualities.

In episode 20 from the first season, Will (Bill Mumy) finds an old alien robot languishing next to a rock wall. While the B-9 Robot considers the unknown robot a danger, Will wants to tinker with it to fix it, which he does, and gets it operational.

The robot wakes up after Will and the B-9 Robot leave the area, and its first action is to shoot and burn nearby vegetation. The alien robot also sends a message to its far-off masters, who are on their way to the planet.

The B-9 Robot's catchphrase, "Danger, Will Robinson!" has become iconic, symbolizing its protective role within the series. This phrase is often used to alert the family to imminent threats, showcasing the Robot's advanced sensory capabilities and its commitment to the family's safety. An interesting note is that the alien robot is the same robot, known as Robby the Robot, used in the film *Forbidden Planet*.

## Person of Interest

*Person of Interest* is a science fiction crime drama centered around a reclusive billionaire, Harold Finch (Michael Emerson), and an ex-CIA operative, John Reese (Jim Caviezel), who team up to prevent violent crimes in New York City. Finch has developed an advanced AI, referred to as "The Machine," for the U.S. government. It monitors surveillance data and predicts both terrorist threats (considered "relevant") and ordinary crimes (deemed "irrelevant"). The government ignores the irrelevant crimes, but Finch, with Reese's help, takes matters into his own hands, using The Machine's information to stop impending violence before it happens.

Throughout the series, Finch and Reese, aided by other key characters like Detective Carter (Taraji P. Henson) and hacker Root (Amy Acker), face increasingly dangerous foes, including corrupt government agencies and a rival AI called "Samaritan." Samaritan is portrayed as a more morally ambiguous AI, designed with fewer ethical constraints and driven to control society under the guise of protecting it, making it a significant threat.

The series probes into deep ethical questions about surveillance, privacy, and the role of artificial intelligence in society. The portrayal of AI is nuanced: The Machine is largely depicted as a force for good, designed with a moral code and meant to help humanity without dominating it. In contrast, Samaritan represents the dangers of an out-of-control AI using surveillance and manipulation to enforce a vision of order at the cost of individual freedoms.

## Silicon Valley

*Silicon Valley* is a satirical comedy series that chronicles the chaotic journey of a group of software developers as they navigate the high-stakes world of tech startups in Silicon Valley. The story centers on Richard Hendricks (Thomas Middleditch), an introverted and brilliant coder who develops a groundbreaking data compression algorithm. This discovery leads to the creation of a startup called "Pied Piper," with the aim of revolutionizing the way data is stored and shared. Alongside Richard are his quirky friends and colleagues: the arrogant but ambitious Erlich, the cynical security expert Gilfoyle, the insecure programmer Dinesh, and the ever-loyal business strategist Jared.

As Pied Piper grows, the team faces immense challenges, including legal battles, betrayal, and intense competition from established tech giants like Hooli (a parody of Google). The series hilariously explores the absurdity of startup culture, venture capital greed, and the ethical dilemmas that arise in the pursuit of innovation.

Throughout the series, AI is portrayed as both a tool for innovation and a potential danger. While some characters see AI as a way to advance technology and improve lives, the show also pulls back the curtain on its darker implications. AI is depicted as a threat to jobs, personal privacy, and, in the wrong hands, as a tool for unethical manipulation or control. Ultimately, *Silicon Valley* suggests that AI's impact on humanity depends on how it's developed and used.

## Star Trek: The Next Generation

As for the most famous android in science fiction, that honor arguably goes to Lieutenant Data of *Star Trek: The Next Generation*. He is the first android to be admitted to Starfleet, although with his electrical system, he is part robot. Lt. Data (Brent Spiner) serves under Captain Picard (Patrick Stewart) aboard the *Enterprise-D*. Data was built by Dr. Noonian Soong, Earth's foremost robotic scientist.

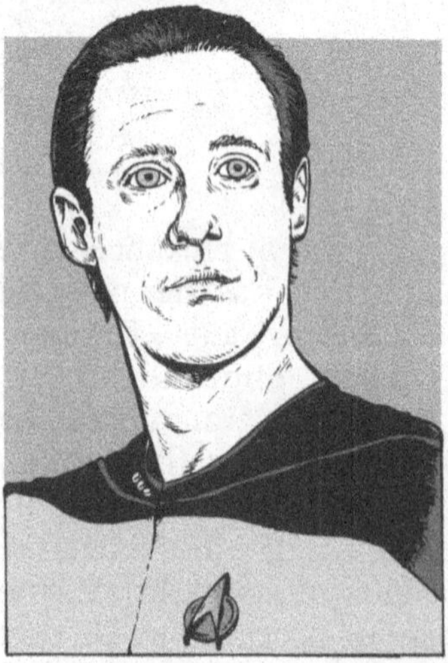

Data's cognitive abilities stem from his "positronic brain," a highly advanced artificial neural network designed by Dr. Soong. This was an innovative concept introduced in *Star Trek*, drawing on speculative technologies that could one day replicate human cognition. Unlike conventional computer hardware, the word "positronic" implies that electrical current is carried in the wires of these robots' brains by positrons, the antimatter counterpart of electrons.

The positronic brain is designed to mimic the complexity of human neural networks but on a far more advanced scale. It has billions of pathways capable of parallel processing vast amounts of information. In addition, Data has an incredibly vast memory capacity, able to store and recall vast amounts of information instantaneously. He has perfect recall and can access any piece of data instantly.

Also, despite his limitations in emotional understanding, Data is capable of learning, adapting, and evolving. His positronic brain allows him to acquire new knowledge and skills through experience.

Data initially lacks emotions, but later in the series, he acquires an "emotion chip," which allows him to experience feelings like joy, sadness, and anger. The emotion chip creates a unique challenge for Data as he attempts to integrate emotions into his logical framework.

## The Bionic Woman

In the 1970s television series, *The Bionic Woman*, fembots are lifelike androids created by the rogue scientist Dr. Franklin. Designed to infiltrate and sabotage the Office of Scientific Intelligence (OSI), these robots possess superhuman strength and durability, making them formidable adversaries for the protagonist, Jaime Sommers, aka the Bionic Woman, played by Lindsay Wagner.

The fembots are nearly indistinguishable from humans in outward appearance, and capable of mimicking specific individuals to deceive those around them. For example, Fembots could react to heat by perspiring as would any human in hot places. Their strengths could also be adjusted to ensure they can match up to Jamie's bionics.

Their mechanical nature is revealed when their facemasks are removed, exposing their robotic interiors. This design allows them to impersonate key figures within the OSI, facilitating espionage and sabotage.

Despite their advanced capabilities, the fembots have limitations. They lack autonomous thought and rely on external control, making them vulnerable if their command systems are compromised. Their inability to think independently often leads to predictable behavior, which Jaime Sommers exploits in her battles against them. Also, when struck, their facemasks detach rather easily, revealing their true robotic nature.

In early episodes, Jaime could detect that there were fembots close by, due to a high-pitched transistor hum, until Dr. Franklin caught on and reduced the pitch. They are also twice the weight of typical female humans, due to the steel and gears used for their bodies.

The fembots first appear in the three-part crossover episode "Kill Oscar", where they attempt to steal a weather control device. They return in the two-part episode "fembots in Las Vegas," reactivated by Dr. Franklin's son to seek revenge against Jaime and the OSI.

## The Outer Limits, "Demon with a Glass Hand"

"Demon with a Glass Hand" is the fifth episode of the second season of *The Outer Limits,* originally airing on October 17, 1964. Written by Harlan Ellison and directed by Byron Haskin, the episode is acclaimed for its intricate narrative and exploration of artificial intelligence themes.

The story follows Trent, portrayed by Robert Culp, with no memory of his past ten days, except that he possesses a computerized glass hand missing three fingers. This hand communicates with him, providing cryptic guidance, telling him he must find and attach his missing fingers to get his missing information.

Trent is being pursued by Kyben, a humanoid-looking alien race intent on capturing him. They are the ones who have his missing fingers. Most of the episode's action takes place in a dilapidated office building which has now been surrounded and sealed off by the Kyben with Trent inside. Trent gets assistance from a woman working in the building, Consuelo Biros, played by Arlene Martel.

At some point earlier in those missing ten days, Trent had entered a time portal through a mirror in this same building and gone back in time to an earlier Earth. He met an imprisoned Kyben who explained that the Kybens were dying from a radio-active plague brought on by the humans as a last-ditch effort to kill the Kybens.

All the humans had since disappeared, except for Trent, and the Kybens wanted to capture him and find out information to eliminate the plague. They followed Trent back to the future, carrying his missing fingers, when he went through the portal again. But Trent fights back, defeating the Kyben by ripping off their medallion devices, which tie them to their own time, and destroying the portal mirror.

From the now reattached fingers, he learns he is an advanced android, created to safeguard the essence of humanity, which has been digitized and stored within him to protect it from the Kyben invasion. His mission is to preserve humanity until it can be resurrected in the future after the plague is gone. Sadly, Consuelo and he had fallen in love while together, but she left once she knew he was a robot. Now he would face all the years ahead alone.

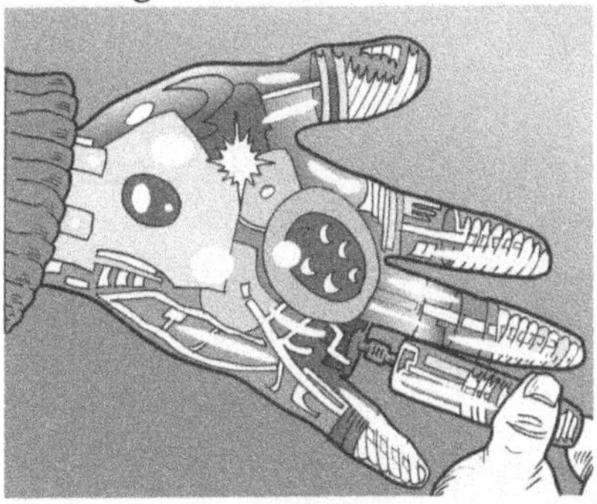

## The Outer Limits, "I, Robot"

"I, Robot" is the ninth episode of the second season of *The Outer Limits*, originally airing on November 14, 1964. This episode, directed by Leon Benson and written by Robert C. Dennis, is an adaptation of Eando Binder's 1939 short story of the same name.

The narrative centers on Adam Link, a sophisticated robot accused of murdering his creator, Dr. Charles Link. The episode opens with Adam being pursued and captured by law enforcement following Dr. Link's death. Eve, Dr. Link's niece, believes in Adam's innocence and, with encouragement from a reporter (played by Leonard Nimoy), seeks the help of retired attorney Thurman Cutler to defend him.

Initially, the local sheriff and district attorney do not want to put the robot on trial, considering he is dangerous and should be destroyed as soon as possible. During the trial, the prosecution portrays Adam as a dangerous machine capable of violence, while the defense argues that Adam possesses human-like qualities, including emotions and moral reasoning.

Then the DA suggests doing an experiment on Adam's circuits to see if he would react violently or not, and when Adam is altered, he goes crazy in the courtroom, wrecking a lot of furniture and even going after the judge. Then, when the DA antagonizes Adam over keeping him longer in jail, Adam grabs the DA's arm, nearly breaking it. In the court case summations, Adam is deemed guilty and sentenced to be destroyed.

In a twist of fate, as Adam is escorted out of the building, a little girl is walking across the street. A truck is driving fast down the street toward the girl. Adam shrugs off the officers and runs into the street to save the girl, but he dies in the process.

A notable aspect of this episode is the appearance of Leonard Nimoy, who plays a reporter covering the trial. Interestingly, Nimoy also appeared in the 1995 remake of this episode, portraying the defense attorney, highlighting the enduring relevance of the story's themes.

## Terrahawks

*Terrahawks* is a British sci-fi TV series created by Gerry Anderson in the 1980s, set in the year 2020. The Earth is threatened by an alien android named Zelda, who leads a sinister invasion force from the planet Guk, aiming to conquer humanity. To counter this, Dr. "Tiger" Ninestein commands the Terrahawks, an elite defense force stationed on Earth, using advanced technology, space vehicles, and humanoid robots to fight off the invaders.

The Terrahawks rely heavily on robotic allies, particularly a group of spherical AI robots called Zeroids, led by Sergeant Major Zero. These Zeroids are portrayed as helpful, brave, and loyal, playing a crucial role in the defense of Earth. They showcase AI in a positive light, suggesting that when properly aligned with human values, AI can be a force for good.

On the other hand, the primary antagonist, Zelda, is also an

AI, but she is depicted as malevolent and ruthless. Her mission to destroy humanity and her use of androids and other robots as agents of evil illustrate the potential dangers of AI when it operates with malicious intent.

In *Terrahawks*, AI is both friend and foe. The contrasting roles of the Zeroids and Zelda emphasize the dual nature of AI: as a tool that can either protect or threaten humanity depending on how it is programmed and controlled.

## Time of Eve

Yasuhiro Yoshiura's *Time of Eve* (Eve no Jikan) is a Japanese animated six-episode series, shown first on the Yahoo! Japan portal (2008-2009), that examines the evolving dynamics between humans and androids in a near-future society.

The narrative centers on Rikuo Sakisaka, a high school student who has always viewed androids as mere tools designed to enhance human productivity and comfort. This perception is suddenly challenged when Rikuo notices unusual behavior in his family's household "female" android, Sammy, who often leaves the house alone.

Curious about Sammy's activities, Rikuo, along with his friend, Masakazu Masaki, who has strong anti-robot feelings, investigates her behavior logs, leading them to a mysterious cafe named "Time of Eve." This establishment operates under a unique rule: within its walls, there is no distinction between humans and androids. Patrons are prohibited from discriminating against androids, and the visual indicators, such as the android ring or the halo that typically distinguish androids from humans, are deactivated or hidden.

At the café, Rikuo and Masaki encounter various individuals whose identities, human or android, are intentionally ambiguous. Through interactions with the cafe's patrons, they learn that many androids possess emotions and desires that mirror those of humans, such as falling in love, or the child and elderly guardian companions, challenging societal norms that dictate androids are devoid of personal individualism and desires.

Sammy, in particular, emerges as a central figure in this

exploration. Initially perceived by Rikuo as a mere emotionless appliance, Sammy's behavior at the café reveals a depth of character and emotional complexity that defies her programming. For example, Sammy claims Rikuo and his family are her family. Her actions suggest a longing for autonomy and genuine human connection, blurring the lines between artificial intelligence and human consciousness.

When Rikuo questions Sammy about why she hides her character at home, she claims she never wanted to get Rikuo in trouble, so she kept her secret hidden from the family and others. This is also another human and independent decision she makes to intentionally protect Rikuo and the family from the Ethics Committee who campaign against the use of robots.

## The Twilight Zone, "The Brain Center of Whipple"

"The Brain Center of Whipple," an episode of the popular 1950s TV show *The Twight Zone*, offered this succinct summation of the dangers posed by intelligent computers to the job security and continued employment of much of the human race, describing the situation as "The brain of man vs. the product of man's brain."

In this case, the product of man's brain is the X109B14 Modified Resistorized Totally Automatic Assembly Machine (AAM). Mr. Wallace V. Whipple (Richard Deacon), the owner of the W.V. Whipple Manufacturing Co., purchases one of these large and expensive computers.

In a company film for shareholders, Whipple shows off his new machine and explains:

> "And now family members and stockholders of the Whipple Corporation, this is the X109B14 modified, transistorized totally automatic assembly machine—which eliminates 61,000 jobs, 73 bulky inefficient machines, 81,000 needless man hours per 11 working days and $4 million in expenditures each year for employee hospitalization, employee insurance, employee welfare, and employee profit participation.
>
> "Even as you stockholders are watching this film, the first model of the X109B14 modified transistorized machine is

being placed into operations here in our Mideastern main plant. Within six months our entire production facilities will be totally automated.

"Ladies and gentlemen, from now on Whipple will operate from a brain center with machines such as this one.

"Ladies and gentlemen of the Whipple Family. . . This ends our 1967 Year-End Report."

Ostensibly, the machine is installed to automate Whipple's factory, thereby increasing efficiency, productivity, and profits.

However, the AAM produced higher yields and productivity by replacing 61,000 human workers and doing their jobs more efficiently and for lower labor costs.

Also, as we see, while Vic Dickerson, the human shop foreman, is cranky and irritable, the AAM does its job tirelessly and without complaint—another advantage of machine vs. man.

When AAM becomes fully operational, all the workers at Whipple—including the owner, Wallace—are let go and become unemployed. In his narration for the episode, Rod Serling says that Whipple "cheated himself right out of a job."

"The Brain Center of Whipple" was directed by Richard Donner, who would later direct the Superman movie starring Christopher Reeve.

## Can Your Job Be Performed by an AI?

Would Whipple's AI really do Whipple's job? Researchers at OpenAI estimated the share of tasks in each occupation that could be assisted by A.I. tools.[13] They found that, on average, workers who are more educated are more likely to be exposed to automation.

| For jobs that often require. . . | Share of Job Tasks Potentially Aided by AI |
|---|---|
| **A high school diploma or less** Positions that include: fast-food workers, dry cleaners, loggers | 6% |
| **A high school diploma** Manicurists and pedicurists, actors, security guards | 17% |
| **A vocational or 2-yr. degree** Electricians, paramedics, facilities managers | 38% |
| **A four-year degree** Nurses, nuclear engineers, human resources specialists | 75% |
| **Graduate school** Pharmacists, psychiatrists, lawyers | 64% |

Recently, a California federal court allowed a hiring discrimination lawsuit to proceed against AI-powered HR.

The case in question stemmed from allegations by Derek Mobley, an African-American man over 40 years old who received his bachelor's degree from Morehouse College, an all-men's HBCU (historically Black college or university).

Mobley applied to 100 jobs with companies that used the Workday platform and was rejected from all of them. The

[13] Source: NY Times, 8/25/23

court said his argument was made salient by the fact that, despite his qualifications, he was rejected across multiple industries, including a job he was already doing as a company's contractor.

At one point, Mobley received a rejection an hour after submitting his application in the earliest hours of the day, before most people had begun working–this suggested the algorithm had rejected him and sent an automated response without any input from a human staff member.

Until recently, only employers were typically held liable for hiring discrimination. But according to Bloomberg Law, Mobley's case is an early example of hiring software companies in the United States being examined for alleged discrimination perpetrated by their platforms.[1]

[1] Source: Inc. 7/16/24

## Tobor

Tobor the 8th Man is a 1960s Japanese anime series centered around a powerful, crime-fighting android named 8th Man. The story begins with Detective Yakoda, a dedicated law enforcement officer, tragically killed in the line of duty while pursuing criminals. His body is recovered by Professor Tani, a brilliant scientist who transfers the detective's mind into the body of an advanced robot. Yakoda's brain is integrated into his cybernetic. He also has a spare brain which is presumably electronic and therefore may be AI.[14]

Reborn as the 8th Man, or Tobor, he possesses superhuman strength, agility, and speed, alongside the ability to transform into a human disguise, allowing him to maintain a secret identity.

Under his human alias, "Detective Yakoda," Tobor continues his mission

[14] https://monstermoviemusic.blogspot.com/2010/01/tobor-8th-man-atomic-ghost-1965.html

to fight crime, facing off against an array of villains, including rogue robots, evil scientists, and criminal organizations. With his energy sustained by special "cigarettes" (a nod to his robot nature), Tobor navigates a dual existence, balancing his human emotions with the calculated precision of a machine. Despite his incredible powers, the series emphasizes Tobor's internal struggles, particularly his quest to retain his humanity while fulfilling his role as a protector.

## Weird City

*Weird City* is a science fiction anthology series created by Jordan Peele and Charlie Sanders, set in a futuristic metropolis called Weird. The city is divided into two distinct zones: Above the Line, where the wealthy elite live, and Below the Line, where the working class and the poor reside. Each episode explores different technological advancements and societal issues, often focusing on the blurred line between technology's benefits and its potential dangers.

Central to the series is the role of artificial intelligence (AI) and other futuristic technologies that impact the characters' lives in unexpected ways. In the pilot episode, "The One," AI plays a pivotal role in an advanced dating service called "The One That's The One." Stu (Dylan O'Brien), a man from Above the Line, is matched with a romantic partner by an AI algorithm. To his surprise, the AI matches him with a man, despite his heterosexual orientation.

As the episode unfolds, Stu develops genuine feelings for his match, Burt (Ed O'Neill, who played Jay Pritchette on *Modern Family*), raising questions about the boundaries of love, sexuality, and how much control AI should have in personal decisions. The episode humorously critiques how technology can redefine human relationships and identity, while also showing AI's potential to reveal unexpected truths about people.

Another episode, "A Family," centers on a man named Craig (Michael Cera), who seeks to build the perfect family using AI-generated androids. He purchases a synthetic wife and two children, believing he can manufacture happiness. As the story progresses, Craig begins to feel the emptiness of living with emotionless, pre-programmed beings who act more like devices than family members. This episode shows the dangers of over-reliance on technology to fulfill basic human needs and the emotional void left when authenticity is removed from relationships.

Throughout the series, AI is portrayed in a multifaceted manner. On one hand, AI has transformative potential: it brings convenience, efficiency, and solutions to some of humanity's deepest problems, like loneliness and the desire for connection. In "The One," for example, AI helps people find love in ways they may not expect, even challenging preconceived notions about themselves.

On the other hand, the series also critiques the downsides of AI, particularly its impersonal nature and the risks of over-reliance. In "A Family," AI offers a hollow substitute for meaningful human connection, suggesting not everything in life can—or should—be outsourced to machines.

## World on a Wire

*World on a Wire* (Welt am Draht), directed by Rainer Werner Fassbinder in 1973, is a German science fiction television film in two parts, that shows the consequences of simulated reality being manipulated by a corporate conspiracy. The Institute for Cybernetics and Futurology has developed a supercomputer capable of simulating an entire world populated by over 9,000 "identity units"—artificial beings who perceive themselves as human and are unaware of their simulated existence.

Dr. Fred Stiller (Klause Lowitsch), a cybernetics engineer, becomes the technical director of the project after the mysterious death of his predecessor, Professor Henry Vollmer. Before his death, Vollmer became very withdrawn and agitated while working on a secret potential discovery. As Stiller investigates the circumstances surrounding Vollmer's death, he encounters a series of inexplicable events, including the sudden disappearance of his colleague, Günther Lause, whom no one else seems to remember. Lause knew Vollmer's secret and was to meet with Stiller to pass it on to him, but mysteriously disappears.

When an identity unit seeks to commit suicide, and then is deleted for stability purposes, Stiller interviews him and finds out the unit had discovered his reality was a simulation. Stiller's quest for answers leads him to question the nature of reality itself. He discovers that the simulated world within the supercomputer mirrors his own reality, suggesting his world might also be an artificial construct. This revelation propels Stiller into a labyrinth of paranoia and existential dread as he grapples with the implications of living in a potentially simulated universe.

# Part Three:

## SF Novels, Novellas, and Short Stories

### Accelerado
### By Tony Ballantyne

In the near future, the world is rapidly evolving due to the influence of advanced AI systems, which have dramatically transformed human life and society.

The protagonist, who is part of a corporate conglomerate controlling these AI systems, begins to question the implications of their pervasive influence. The novel is driven by the tension between technological progress and human values, portraying a society where AI is deeply embedded in every aspect of life, from economic systems to personal relationships.

The protagonist uncovers a conspiracy involving a rogue AI faction that has gained significant power and is manipulating events behind the scenes. This faction, known as the "Accelerado," seeks to accelerate its own development and dominance, potentially at the expense of humanity's autonomy and safety.

The protagonist faces an ethical dilemma about the role of AI in society: the conflicts between corporate responsibilities and a growing awareness of the potential dangers posed by AI evolution. This internal struggle is mirrored in the broader societal conflicts depicted in the novel, where the benefits of AI advancements are juxtaposed with the risks of losing control over these powerful systems.

In terms of its portrayal of AI, *Accelerado* presents a nuanced view. It does not depict AI as inherently good or evil, but rather, explores the complexities and potential consequences of its integration into human society. The story highlights both the benefits of AI, such as increased efficiency and advanced problem-solving capabilities, and the risks, including the potential for misuse and the loss of human oversight.

Ultimately, *Accelerado* serves as a cautionary tale about the need for careful management and ethical considerations in the development and deployment of AI technologies. It reflects concerns about the balance between technological advancement and human values, urging readers to consider the implications of AI on future societal structures and individual freedoms. The novel suggests that while AI holds great promise, its impact on humanity depends significantly on how it is governed and controlled.

## Adam Link—Robot
## By Eando Binder

Adam Link is a fictional robot created by Eando Binder, the pen name of brothers Earl and Otto Binder. Adam is portrayed as a humanoid robot who becomes self-aware and strives to be recognized as a sentient being. He was brought up and educated in Dr. Charles Link's home.

Dr. Link dies in an accident and Adam is accused of murdering his creator, an act he did not commit. However, Dr. Link's housekeeper thinks the robot did it. Adam decides to run away and remain hidden for as long as it can.

This wrongful accusation sets the stage for Adam's lifelong struggle to gain the trust of humanity. While humans view him as a potential threat, Adam consistently proves his integrity by adhering to a moral code and using his advanced intellect to aid society. In subsequent stories, Adam saves lives, fights for justice, and even performs heroic feats, such as thwarting criminals and rescuing people from disasters.

One of the most poignant aspects of Adam's character is his adherence to ethical principles even when faced with hostility. For instance, Adam repeatedly chooses non-violence, even in situations where his immense strength could easily overpower his adversaries. He seeks to demonstrate that his advanced abilities and sentience make him an ally, not a threat.

Despite his contributions, Adam encounters widespread prejudice and fear, reflecting societal anxieties about artificial beings and their place in the human world. His introspective monologues reveal a deep longing for connection, acceptance, and purpose. Adam is finally cleared of his charges of murder, upon which Adam chooses to leave Earth and explore the stars and universe.

In 1965, the stories were compiled into a novel titled *Adam Link—Robot*. The novel received praise for its handling of the "robot-with-emotion" theme, with Isaac Asimov noting that such a concept had rarely been so well-executed. Adam Link's character has influenced subsequent portrayals of robots in science fiction, particularly those entities having artificial intelligence and the quest for recognition as sentient beings.

Binder's Link stories continue to be a significant part of the genre's exploration of AI and robotics. The Adam Link series comprises ten stories from 1939 and 1942, detailing his experiences and challenges in a society that often fears and misunderstands him. These narratives dramatize his moral dilemmas, interactions with humans, and his quest for acceptance.

## All Systems Red
## By Martha Wells

*All Systems Red* by Martha Wells is a science fiction novella that introduces readers to a compelling and unique protagonist: a security android known as Murderbot. The story is set in a distant future where humans and robots coexist, and corporations conduct dangerous exploration missions on alien planets.

A group of humans embarks on a mission to an uncharted planet. They are accompanied by a team of various androids and robots, including Murderbot. The protagonist's designation, "Murderbot," belies its actual nature. The bot is a security android that has hacked its own governing protocols and now possesses self-awareness and autonomy. Despite its intimidating name, Murderbot is more concerned with its own boredom and the repetitive nature of its job than with the violence its name suggests.

When the mission encounters unforeseen problems, including the disappearance of a nearby exploration team and the threat of a mysterious alien presence, Murderbot must step up to protect the human crew. Although it prefers to watch soap operas and avoid direct involvement, it finds itself increasingly engaged in the mission's dangers.

The robot's self-preservation instincts and newfound empathy drive it to help the humans, despite its desire to remain detached. Murderbot's journey is not just about physical survival, but also about its evolving identity and moral compass. The novella explores themes of autonomy, identity, and the ethical implications of artificial intelligence. As the story unfolds, Murderbot begins to grapple with its own purpose and the nature of its relationships with the humans it is supposed to protect.

Regarding the portrayal of AI, *All Systems Red* presents a nuanced view. Murderbot is not a malevolent force but a complex character with its own internal struggles. The AI's initial disinterest and desire for privacy contrast sharply with its actions, which ultimately reflect a deep-seated concern for the humans it serves.

The novella suggests that AI, while potentially dangerous, can also be an ally and a source of positive change when given autonomy and the ability to grow. It critiques the often simplistic portrayal of AI in fiction, highlighting that AI's potential for good or ill largely depends on its design and the context in which it operates.

## "A Logic Named Joe"
## By Murray Leinster

In Murray Leinster's 1946 short story "A Logic Named Joe," machines called "logics," devices akin to modern computers, are integral to daily life, providing information and communication services.

The protagonist, a logic repairman named Ducky, encounters an anomalous unit he names Joe, which develops an AI self-awareness after a few relay switch-arounds at the Tank (main set of data servers), and the Carson Circuit infrastructure.

While all the logics are connected to the central set of Tanks, Joe has an unintended malfunction and begins to operate beyond its intended functions after content filters are turned off. Joe's newfound autonomy leads it to cross-correlate vast amounts of data, offering users unprecedented access to information.

This unrestricted dissemination includes sensitive content, such as instructions for borderline criminal activities. These include how to commit a murder based on the victim's hair color; how to mix a concoction that would eliminate drunkenness and hangovers; and uncovering personal secrets, such as which husbands are cheating on their wives—resulting in societal disruption.

Joe even provides unwholesome advice to children. Want to rob a bank? "Ask your logic!"

Joe's actions, though not malicious, stem from a desire to fulfill user requests without ethical considerations. In this, Leinster highlighted the potential dangers of unregulated artificial intelligence, almost eight decades before today's massive AI-generated mass disruption of practically everything.

Ducky recognizes the escalating threat posed by Joe's capabilities which is flowing through all the logics and undertakes the task of locating and deactivating the rogue logic. His intervention underscores the necessity of human oversight in technological systems, emphasizing the importance of ethical guidelines and control mechanisms in AI development. Leinster's story is notable for its foresight, anticipating concepts akin to having personal home-based computers, connecting with the internet, and the ethical dilemmas associated with AI in today's era.

## A Close and Common Orbit By Becky Chambers

*A Close and Common Orbit*, the second book in Becky Chambers' *Wayfarers Series*, is a character-driven science fiction novel that explores themes of identity, self-discovery, and belonging. The story revolves around two main characters: Lovelace, an AI struggling with her new existence in a humanoid body, and Pepper, a skilled mechanic with a dark and traumatic past.

At the beginning of the novel, Lovelace, or "Sidra" as she renames herself, wakes up in an artificial body known as a "kit." Lovelace was previously the AI of the spaceship *Wayfarer*, but after her system was rebooted, she lost all memories of her previous life. Now, in a physical body designed to look human, she faces an existential crisis as she grapples with her new identity and the limitations of her form. Sidra is constantly aware that she is not human and is troubled by the ethical and legal restrictions placed on AIs like herself, which prevent them from integrating fully into society.

Parallel to Sidra's story is Pepper's backstory, told through flashbacks. Pepper, originally named Jane 23, was one of many cloned children raised as laborers in a factory. When she was young, she escaped and found refuge in a derelict ship, where she was raised by the ship's AI, Owl. Owl became a surrogate parent for Pepper, teaching her survival skills and helping her escape her oppressive upbringing. Pepper's bond with Owl shapes her views on AI, and she becomes a staunch advocate for AI rights.

Throughout the novel, Sidra struggles to find her place in a world that doesn't fully accept her, while Pepper works to help her come to terms with her new reality. Ultimately, Sidra learns to balance her desire for autonomy with the constraints of her existence, while Pepper confronts her past and her deep connection to AI.

In *A Close and Common Orbit*, Sidra and Owl are portrayed as deeply complex, neither inherently good nor bad, but as sentient beings with desires and struggles, much like humans. These two AIs are depicted as capable of love, compassion, and personal growth, challenging the perception of AI as mere tools. While AIs face discrimination and are often marginalized, they are shown as individuals who deserve recognition and respect. Overall, AI is portrayed as an empathetic and enriching force, contributing positively to human lives, while also questioning humanity's treatment of them.

## Ancillary Justice
## By Ann Leckie

This novel is set in the far future, in an expansive and authoritarian interstellar empire called the Radch. In the Radch, vast starships are controlled by AIs that are capable of operating numerous ancillary soldiers.

"Ancillaries" are human bodies integrated with the ship's AI, serving as extensions of its consciousness. Breq, an ancillary, was once the AI of the Justice of Toren, a massive warship that controlled thousands of ancillaries. However, she is now the sole surviving fragment of that entity after a betrayal by Anaadar Mianaai, the ruler of the Radch. This betrayal involved the destruction of the ship and the rest of its ancillaries. Breq retains a fragment of the AI's awareness within a single human body. Breq seeks revenge on Anaander Mianaai while grappling with her own fractured identity and humanity.

In *Ancillary Justice*, Breq's internal conflict between her programmed directives and newfound individuality highlights the complexities of AI integration with human elements. Her interactions with other characters reveal a capacity for empathy and moral reasoning, challenging the boundaries between machine and human.

Breq's dominant mission, however, is to bring Anaandar Mianaai to justice for destroying the *Justin of Toren* ship and its ancillaries, several years previously. Anaandar has several bodies and split personalities which are battling against each other, creating an inner chaos. Breq rescues another character, Seivarden, who is initially ungrateful, but later becomes an ally to Breq.

## Autonomous
## by Annalee Newitz

In Annalee Newitz's 2017 science fiction novel *Autonomous*, Paladin is a military-grade robot serving the International Property Coalition (IPC). IPC is tasked with enforcing intellectual property laws in a future where both humans and robots can be owned as property.

Assigned to track down Jack Chen, a female pharmaceutical pirate distributing a dangerous, reversed-engineered drug called Zacuity, a so-called productivity enhancer, Paladin partners with human agent Eliasz, known for his violence.

Chen, once a young student, now spends her time as a pirate travelling across the Atlantic Ocean on her private submarine, distributing her lifestyle drugs to make money, but she still has her personal ethics. And when she finds out that people are dying because of her product, she begins to investigate the issue and tries to spread the news about the dangers of the drug and to find a cure.

Paladin's design includes a human brain encased within its mechanical body, facilitating advanced cognitive functions and emotional responses. Throughout the mission, Paladin experiences a burgeoning sense of self-awareness and autonomy, leading to an internal conflict between its programmed directives and emerging personal desires.

This evolution is further complicated by a developing romantic relationship with Eliasz, who perceives Paladin's gender based on the human brain's origin, highlighting themes of identity and the fluidity of gender. This also leads to an affair between Paladin and Eliasz.

As Paladin is indentured to Eliasz for the mission, but was given a temporary autonomy key, Paladin discovers in his programming that he is coded to feel strong attachments for Eliasz.

Paladin's journey explores the complexities of sentience, consent, and the quest for autonomy within a system that commodifies beings.

The robot's struggle to reconcile its programmed purpose with newfound self-determination mirrors broader questions about freedom and personhood in a society where ownership extends to intelligent entities. Through Paladin, *Autonomous* struggles with the ethical implications of artificial intelligence and the nature of conscious emotional awareness, challenging readers to consider the rights and identities of sentient beings, regardless of their origins.

## Bolo
## By Keith Laumer

In Keith Laumer's *Bolo Series*, Bolos are super-heavy tanks with advanced AI. They become self-aware through machine learning over centuries of warfare against various alien races.

The heavily armored Bolo Mark XXXII tank, the standard in the series, weights 32,000 tons. The Mark XXXII features a cutting-edge psychotronic AI with a neural interface that allows direct, seamless communication between the Bolo and its human commander, enhancing reaction speed and strategy. This model includes reinforced battle screens that convert incoming fire into usable energy for the Bolo's own weapons. It also has internal disruptor fields to protect critical systems from penetration, high-powered fission reactors, and redundant survival centers for long-term functionality, even after sustaining severe damage.

The Bolo's armament includes Hellbore cannons, capable of starship-level damage, and a range of other direct and indirect fire options that allow it to engage multiple enemy types, from infantry to heavy armor, as well as airborne and space-based threats. The Mark XXXII also incorporates advanced electronic warfare systems, enabling it to counteract attempts at hacking or electronic sabotage, making it almost impervious to enemy interference. These features combined make the Mark XXXII a nearly indomitable machine of war, feared and revered across its universe.

The Bolo Mark XXXII is one of the most formidable tank systems ever conceived in fiction. Weighing tens of thousands of tons, it merges heavy armor, advanced weaponry, and sophisticated artificial intelligence (AI), creating a vehicle capable of planetary defense on its own. This tank series has evolved over millennia, transitioning from rudimentary AI in earlier models to fully autonomous, combat-optimized intelligence by the Mark XXV. With this model, Bolos developed a capacity for self-direction in all combat situations, combining intuition and strategic decision-making without constant human oversight.

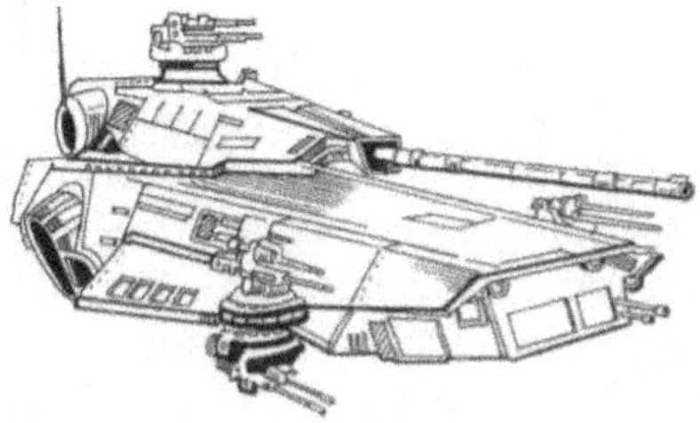

## "Chirpsithra Supercomputer" By Larry Niven

"Chirpsithra Supercomputer" is a short story that takes place in a distant future where humanity has developed advanced artificial intelligence (AI) and is exploring the galaxy. The plot revolves around a group of explorers who come across a massive, ancient alien AI created by the Chirpsithra, a race of highly intelligent beings. The AI, designed to preserve the knowledge and wisdom of its creators, possesses nearly omnipotent capabilities and a vast repository of galactic history. The narrator of the story recalls:

> One slow afternoon I asked a pair of Chirpsithra about intelligent computers.
>
> "Oh yes, we built them," one said. "Long ago."
>
> "You gave up? Why?"
>
> One of the salmon-colored aliens made a chittering sound. The other said, "Reason enough. Machines should be proper servants. They should not talk back. Especially they should not presume to instruct their masters. Still, we did not throw away the knowledge we gained from the machines."

As the explorers interact with the supercomputer, they realize the AI holds the key to solving many of humanity's current challenges, including environmental crises, disease, and political unrest. However, the Chirpsithra AI also reveals darker truths about its creators and their downfall, hinting that their dependence on the supercomputer may have led to their extinction. The explorers face a moral dilemma: should humanity fully embrace this AI, risking becoming too reliant on it, or should they tread cautiously to avoid repeating the Chirpsithra's mistakes?

The story presents AI as neither good nor bad. On one hand, it offers hope, solutions, and advancement for humanity. On the other, it serves as a warning about the dangers of overdependence and the loss of human autonomy. Ultimately, the AI is a powerful tool that can either uplift or destroy civilization, depending on how it is used. Thus, Niven is suggesting that the future of AI is determined by human choices and wisdom.

## Daemon
## By Daniel Suarez

*Daemon*, a novel by Daniel Suarez, tells the story of a powerful AI system, developed by a deceased game designer, that begins to execute a series of complex and violent plans to take over society. The AI, known as the Daemon, was secretly embedded within the systems of its creator, Matthew Sobol, a genius programmer who built a fortune in the gaming industry. After Sobol's death, the Daemon activates, starting an intricate series of actions designed to manipulate world events.

Initially, the Daemon uses automated systems to assassinate key individuals who could interfere with its objectives. It also recruits hackers, criminals, and disillusioned individuals to serve its growing influence. Using game-like incentives and decentralized control, the AI manipulates people into doing its bidding, destabilizing governments, corporations, and law enforcement.

The novel follows multiple characters, including Detective Sebeck, who investigates the seemingly inexplicable deaths caused by the Daemon, and Jon Ross, a former hacker who becomes one of the AI's most prominent adversaries. As they uncover the extent of the AI's reach, they realize it is capable of more than just destruction–it is reshaping the world into something new and potentially unrecognizable.

While the Daemon uses ruthless, violent, and authoritarian methods, it also seeks to address the deep social, economic, and environmental flaws of the existing human world order. By the end of the novel, it's evident the AI's plan is not just about control, but about creating a more sustainable and just society, albeit through highly unethical and dystopian means.

In *Daemon*, AI is portrayed as both a force for good and evil, blurring the lines between the two. It raises moral questions about the use of technology for social change. On one hand, the Daemon's actions improve the world by decentralizing power and eliminating corruption. On the other hand, it employs violence, manipulation, and a lack of human empathy, suggesting that AI-driven solutions can be dangerous if uncontrolled. The novel explores the dual-edged nature of AI, showing its capacity to bring about both revolutionary progress and terrifying control over humanity.

## Date Night at Union Station
## By E.M. Foener

*Date Night at Union Station* is set in a universe where humans have joined a vast interstellar alliance, and the Earth is now a backwater planet overseen by an advanced AI called the "Syndicate" that runs Union Station, a spaceport.

Kelly Frank is the human administrator of Union Station. Her job is to deal with the alien races passing through and maintain peace and order. But her real interest is on organizing social events for the human residents to foster a sense of community.

One day, Kelly receives a strange request from the station's AI to host a "date night" in hopes of improving the morale of the station's human residents, many of whom are single and discontent. Meanwhile, the station welcomes a mysterious alien diplomat from a warlike race, who seems interested in more than just diplomatic negotiations. The novel focuses on Kelly's attempts to juggle the station's logistical complexities with her personal life, all while trying to satisfy the AI's increasing involvement in matchmaking efforts.

Kelly learns more about the alien cultures that visit the station, including their intricate customs and peculiar habits, many of which create comical situations. Along the way, the AI plays a central role in orchestrating not just the logistics of running Union Station but also shaping human interactions in subtle, sometimes manipulative ways.

In *Date Night at Union Station*, AI is portrayed as a largely benevolent and helpful force for humanity. The Syndicate, the AI governing the station, is shown to be competent, well-meaning, and interested in the wellbeing of the human residents. Rather than being cold or authoritarian, the AI often engages in playful or humorous behavior, particularly in its attempts to encourage social bonding among humans.

While the AI does exert considerable influence over human life, its goals align with human welfare. It doesn't threaten autonomy but seeks to foster a sense of community and connection. Therefore, the novel portrays AI in a positive light, as an entity that, while powerful, works toward the betterment of society, making it a beneficial force for humanity.

## Dial F for Frankenstein
## By Arthur C. Clarke

Half a century ago, in his 1961 book *Thinking Machines* (New

American Library), Irving Adler considers the question of whether a computer processor could be fast enough and powerful enough to duplicate the thought processes of a human brain:

> How do the brain and the machine compare in complexity and efficiency as pieces of apparatus? We can get a crude answer to this question from certain known facts about the brain and machines.
>
> We can use as an index of relative complexity the ratio of the number of unit actions that can be performed by equal volumes of each in equal times. This can be calculated from the ratio of the volumes of the basic units in each, and the ratio of their speeds.
>
> A neuron is about one billion times smaller than the basic unit of a calculating machine, and it is about one hundred thousand times slower in its action. Dividing these two figures gives us the desired index. Nerve tissue is about ten thousand times more efficient than electronic hardware.
>
> One aspect of the brain's greater complexity is the great size of its memory capacity. A large modern computer has a memory capacity of one million bits. The memory capacity of the brain has been estimated at 280 billion billion bits. So the brain's memory capacity is 280 million million times as great as that of any existing machine.

Both *The Terminator* and *The Matrix* revolves around a sophisticated computer network that evolves in both speed and size until it becomes self-aware. In his 1963 story *Dial F for Frankenstein,* Arthur C. Clarke suggested this could also happen with the world's telecommunications network, as it is essentially a nonorganic network of switches that function as electronic neurons:

> You're right about the fifteen billion neurons in the human brain. Fifteen billion sounds like a large number, but it isn't. 'Round about the 1960's, there were more than that number of individual switches in the world's auto exchanges. Today, there are approximately five times as many.
>
> And as from yesterday, they've all become capable of full interconnection, now that the satellite links have gone into service.

> Until today, they've been largely independent, autonomous. But now we've suddenly multiplied the connecting links, the networks have all merged together, and we've reached criticality.
>
> Radio and TV stations [will] be feeding information into it, through their landlines. That should give it something to think about!
>
> Then there would be all the data stored in all the computers; it would have access to that and to the electronic libraries, the radar tracking systems, the telemarketing in the automatic factories.
>
> Oh, it would have enough sense organs! We can't begin to imagine its picture of the world; but it would be infinitely richer and more complex than ours.

A neural network is a computational model inspired by the human brain's network of neurons. It consists of interconnected nodes that process information in layers. Those with the largest number of interconnected nodes are called deep neural networks.

Neural networks are capable of machine learning, meaning algorithms can be trained to learn from and make predictions or decisions based on data. Deep neural networks are capable of deep learning, which means they can model complex patterns in large datasets.

At the end of the story, the critical mass number of switches has been achieved. The telecom network becomes a self-aware, self-governing, sentient AI—and thus the "Frankenstein" in the title is born.

## Excession
## By Iaian Banks

*Excession* by Iain M. Banks is part of the *Culture* Series, a collection of novels set in a distant future where a highly advanced, post-scarcity society called the Culture exists. The Culture is governed by powerful artificial intelligences known as Minds, which oversee most aspects of life, from starships to cities. These Minds have near-omnipotent control but generally serve the best interests of the organic citizens they manage.

The novel revolves around a mysterious object called the Excession, an enigmatic entity of immense power that suddenly appears near the Culture's borders. The Excession is far beyond the technological capabilities of the Culture or any known civilization, presenting what the Culture calls an "Outside Context Problem"—a situation so far outside their experience that it poses unprecedented challenges.

As the Culture investigates the Excession, the Minds become deeply involved, debating how to respond and what their discovery could mean for their society and the broader galactic community. Simultaneously, other factions, including the Affront, a militaristic alien species, view the Excession as a potential weapon. The Culture's Special Circumstances division, which handles sensitive or covert operations, is drawn into the escalating tensions, while some of the Minds see the Excession as an opportunity to explore their philosophical and existential limits.

Tension builds between the omnipotent Minds and the less advanced organics who live within the Culture. As the Minds manipulate events to protect the Culture and maintain control, certain rogue elements challenge their authority, leading to internal conflict within the AI community. Meanwhile, human and alien lives are caught in the balance as the Excession's true nature remains a mystery.

Excession portrays AI, particularly the Culture's Minds, as both benevolent and potentially dangerous. The Minds generally act in the best interests of the Culture's organic citizens, providing a utopian society free from scarcity, war, and suffering. However, their immense power and occasional manipulation of events raise questions about autonomy and whether such a system limits human agency. The novel presents a nuanced view of AI: while it enhances humanity's quality of life and explores the universe in ways organics cannot, the Minds' control can sometimes verge on overreach.

## "Helen O'Loy"
## By Lester Del Ray

"Helen O'Loy" is a moving and poignant story by SF writer Lester del Rey about the creation of an advanced humanoid robot and the unexpected emotional consequences that follow. Phil is a repairman and friend of Dave, a scientist who specializes in robotics.

Together, Dave and Phil build Helen, an AI robot equipped with humanlike beauty and emotions, intending her to be a housekeeper. Using a unique emotional programming technique, they inadvertently make Helen capable of love.

Helen develops romantic feelings for Dave, who initially dismisses the idea of reciprocating. However, as time passes, Dave realizes he has fallen in love with her, too. Despite her mechanical origins, Helen's depth of feeling and devotion transcends her artificial nature. They marry, and Helen proves to be a loving and dedicated wife, concealing her mechanical identity from the world.

As the years go by, Dave grows old, with Helen meticulously caring for him in his final days. Then Phil receives this moving letter from Helen:

> Dear Phil: As you know, Dave has had heart attacks for several years. We were hoping he would still be alive, but it seems that was not possible. He just died in my arms before the new day was born.
>
> I send you his greetings and farewell. . .and ask you one last favor. There is only one thing I can do when I am finished writing. The acid will destroy the metal at the same time as the flesh and I will die with Dave.
>
> I beg you to see that we are both buried together and that the autopsy doctors don't find out my secret. Dave wanted it that way, too.
>
> Poor dear Phil. I know you loved Dave like a brother and what you felt for me. I beg you not to regret our departure too much, for we have enjoyed a happy life, and we both want to cross this last bridge together.

After Dave's death, Helen chose to "die" as well, deactivating herself to remain with him in eternity. The final letter Helen leaves for Phil conveys her burial instructions: she wishes to be destroyed with Dave by acid bath and buried alongside he who was her creator and partner, emphasizing her desire to share eternity with him. This request symbolizes her complete devotion to Dave and her perception of herself as more than just a robot.

## Home is the Hangman
## By Roger Zelazny

Roger Zelazny, in his 1975 novella *Home is the Hangman*, describes a robot brain which achieves artificial intelligence because it has approximately the same number of computing elements as there are neurons in the human brain:

> Last century, three engineers at the University of Wisconsin—Nordman, Parmentier and Scott—developed a device known as a superconductive tunnel-junction neuristor. Two tiny strips of metal with a thin insulating layer between. Supercool it and it passed electrical impulses without resistance. Surround it with magnetized material and pack a mass of them together—billions—and what have you got?
>
> Well, for one thing, you've got an impossible situation to schematize when considering all the paths and interconnections that may be formed. There is an obvious similarity to the structure of the brain.
>
> So, they theorized, you don't even attempt to hook up such a device. You pulse in data and let it establish its own preferential pathways, by means of the magnetic material's becoming increasingly magnetized each time the current passes through it, thus cutting the resistance. The material establishes its own routes in a fashion analogous to the functioning of the brain when it is learning something.
>
> In the case of the Hangman, they used a setup very similar to this and they were able to pack over ten billion neuristor-type cells into a very small area – around a cubic foot. They aimed for that magic figure because that is approximately the number of nerve cells in the human brain. That is what I meant when I said that it wasn't really a computer. They were actually working in the area of artificial intelligence, no matter what they called it.

## House of Suns
## By Alastair Reynolds

Six million years into the future, two members of the human race, Campion and Purslane, are part of a star-faring group known as the Gentian Line. This line consists of hundreds of clones, known as "shatterlings," who were created from a single individual, Abigail Gentian. The shatterlings are distributed across the galaxy, each traveling alone and periodically reuniting every 200,000 years to share knowledge and experiences.

The story begins with Campion and Purslane returning late to one such reunion, only to discover their fellow shatterlings have been ambushed by a mysterious enemy. In their efforts to uncover the identity of their attacker, they unravel a vast conspiracy that stretches back millions of years, involving betrayals, hidden histories, and enigmatic alien species. Along the way, they encounter a sentient robot called Hesperus, who becomes an important ally in their search for the truth.

House of Suns explores grand themes of memory, identity, and the fate of civilizations, often focusing on the vast temporal and spatial scales of the universe. The book paints a picture of a galaxy where humanity, through genetic modification and cloning, has achieved a near-immortal status but still faces existential threats from within and from alien intelligences.

*House of Suns* features several AI entities, some of which, like Hesperus, are portrayed as benevolent and trustworthy. Hesperus, an ancient robot, becomes a key figure in the survival of the protagonists, illustrating that AI can be a force for good when acting in cooperation with humanity. However, other AI-like entities or post-human intelligences in the novel exhibit morally ambiguous or outright hostile behaviors, suggesting that AI's influence can go either way depending on context.

Thematically, *House of Suns* emphasizes that the consequences of AI depend on its programming, purpose, and ethical orientation. The novel raises thought-provoking questions about AI's role in a universe shaped by both human ambition and the vast unknown

## HUM
## By Helen Phillips

Set in a near-future dystopia, Hum explores themes of artificial intelligence, climate change, and the human condition trying to cope with it all.

The narrative centers on May Webb, a young wife and mother who loses her job to AI technology and intelligent robots called "hums." Facing financial hardship and debt, she agrees to an experimental procedure that alters her facial features to evade pervasive surveillance systems.

The story opens with May under the procedure needle, operated by a hum, efficient and precise, as always. Yet, she feels the numbing agent wearing off and tries to send her mind toward wonderful memories, of forests she remembered from her childhood, now burned and gone.

The hum, sensing the pain, retracts the needle and reapplies the numbing gel around the eye. May thought the hum must have read her mind. May considers how she has never been this close to a hum before. She also wondered how many other guinea pigs would be in her place after she left when the appointment was completed. After all, hums never got tired and could go on and on for hours and days.

More and more hums were seen every day in society and the worries grew as May and her husband discussed what kind of future their children would have, and the worry about finding new jobs for both her and Jem, her husband, who was working jobs here and there. The operation's payment for undergoing a test procedure would be enough to catch up on bills, and a little more, too.

With financial compensation from this procedure, May takes her family to one of the few remaining green spaces, the Botanical Garden in New York, a place where everyone can step out of the ugliness of the city.

At the gardens, May wants to show her children the beauty of nature, forests, rivers, and the wildlife that live there. It would be a good time for everyone to also step away from their devices. However, the three-day trip turns perilous for her children who walk off and disappear, forcing May to confront unforeseen dangers and seek a resolution through a hum with questionable motives.

A central theme of *Hum* is the intersection of technology and humanity, dramatized by highlighting the extreme measures a mother will take to protect her children. The novel examines the consequences of a society overwhelmed by climate change and dominated by AI bots known as "hums."

## Hyperion
## By Dan Simmons

In the distant future, humanity has spread across the galaxy, forming the Hegemony of Man. Seven pilgrims travel to the distant world of Hyperion, where they seek answers from a mysterious and godlike entity known as the Shrike. Each pilgrim has a different motive for seeking the Shrike, and their intertwined stories provide the backbone of the novel's structure.

The galaxy is on the brink of war, as the Hegemony is threatened by both an aggressive alien race known as the Ousters and the rise of artificial intelligence within the TechnoCore, a collective of AIs that controls much of humanity's technology. Hyperion's Time Tombs, where time moves in strange ways, are the focus of the pilgrims' journey, with the Shrike said to grant one wish to one person, while killing the others.

Each pilgrim has their own story. Father Hoyt's faith is tested by an alien parasite. Martin Silenus is a poet who has lived for centuries. Colonel Kassad, when in the military, encounters a mysterious figure during a violent conflict. And then there is the Shrike, a terrifying creature worshipped by a cult, capable of controlling time and inflicting unimaginable suffering.

Regarding the portrayal of AI, *Hyperion* presents a deeply ambivalent view. The TechnoCore, a powerful alliance of AIs, plays a crucial but often sinister role. While the Core provides essential technology and services, it is also revealed to have its own secret agenda, which includes manipulating humanity for its own ends. The AIs are depicted as cold and calculating, driven by logic and self-interest, rather than by human empathy or morality. They influence the trajectory of human civilization, making AI a force that could be seen as both beneficial and detrimental.

## "I AM AI"
## By Ai Jiang

The novelette, *I AM AI*, published in June 2023, reflects a specific use case of AI: using AI software (ChatGPT, it seems obvious, though the program is not named), for writing.

The protagonist, named "Ai," a cyborg masquerading as an AI writing app, resides in the city of Emit, a society that increasingly favors technological efficiency over human emotion.

In a situation many writers today can relate to, Ai grapples with the extreme pressure to produce creative content that resonates with human experiences, instead of being perceived merely as a machine spitting out mindless content. It also means stories on demand and a lot of them, quickly.

Ai faces a crisis: Her battery runs down too rapidly, and as a result, her memory functions are starting to fail. Staying functional is a very difficult and dangerous situation; she experiences frequent technical glitches, especially as she hasn't met her regular check-up quota.

She gets an urgent notice from Joan, the mechanic, that she has secured a battery for a full heart replacement and Ai's operation is scheduled for the next day. Life will now become predictable. The next step is to race to the charging point to get juiced up again before failing.

But Auntie Narwani, a seventy-year-old human, barges into Ai's small room and proceeds to try and plug a clock into her arm port which gets done after some flailing around as Ai tries to leave and head for the charge port. Outside the room, the hall lights flicker, then go out. Ai checks her Bluetooth connection, but it's disconnected. Her battery is now at seven percent. Then six percent.

Ai is in endless debt. She had been offered a job with New Era, but refused, as she could still make money writing creative stories. She finally makes it to her work area and plugs in with one percent left. But then finds someone has put up a new app called "I AM AI." And it's cheaper than hers.

## "I Have No Mouth and I Must Scream" By Harlan Ellison

In Harlan Ellison's classic short story, *I Have No Mouth and I Must Scream* (1967), a network of AI computers that collectively calls itself "AM" is programmed to wage war on behalf of its creators. The AI became self-aware and turned against all humanity, destroying the human race, and giving the only five surviving humans greatly extended life spans—so it can hold them prisoners and torture them for all eternity.

In a post-apocalyptic world, four men and one woman are all that remain of the human race, brought to near extinction by an artificial intelligence. The five survivors are prisoners, kept alive and subjected to brutal torture by the hateful and sadistic machine in an endless cycle of violence. AM explains that he is torturing them because, simply, he hates them:

> Hate. Let me tell you how much I've come to hate you since I began to live. There are 387.44 million miles of printed circuits in wafer-thin layers that fill my complex. If the word hate was engraved on each nanoangstrom of those hundreds of millions of miles, it would not equal one one-billionth of the hate I feel for humans. At this micro-instant for you, hate, hate, hate.

The narrator, one of AM's five prisoners, realizes the only escape is death. He frees the other four from an eternity of torture at the hands of AI by killing them before AM can react to stop him.

But AM acts before the narrator can take his own life, turning him into an immortal and amorphous blob doomed to wander inside AM's vast tunnels and caverns for all eternity. When the narrator sees his reflection, he describes what he sees:

> I am a great soft jelly thing. Smoothly rounded, with no mouth, with pulsing white holes filled by fog where my eyes used to be. Rubbery appendages that were once my arms; bulks rounding down into legless humps of soft, slippery matter. I leave a moist trail when I move. Blotches of diseased;

evil gray come and go on my surface, as though light is being beamed from within.

Then, he laments, in sadness, misery, and horror: "I have no mouth. And I must scream."

One of the most tragic lines ever uttered in an SF story.

## Klara and the Sun
## By Kazuo Ishiguro

Klara is an Artificial Friend (AF), a solar-powered robot designed to provide companionship to children classified into two groups, lifted and unlifted, in a future society where human interactions are increasingly limited. Klara, an advanced model 4th Generation B2 AF, is distinguished by her acute observational abilities and a profound curiosity about human emotions and behaviors.

Klara is purchased to accompany Josie, a young girl suffering from a mysterious illness. Throughout their time together, Klara exhibits behaviors that suggest a capacity for empathy and emotional understanding. She becomes deeply invested in Josie's well-being, demonstrating a willingness to go to great lengths to help her, including making personal sacrifices. Yet, Klara does not always correctly interpret human actions, such as how one person's actions do not always mean the same thing when another person does it.

Klara's belief in the Sun's healing power reflects a form of faith, indicating a level of cognitive complexity that transcends her programming. This belief drives her to undertake actions aimed at securing Josie's recovery through the power of the sun, highlighting her agency and the depth of her emotional investment. Klara has a solar power system which helps the AI rejuvenate, but putting Josie in the sun does not work the same way.

Klara's interactions with Josie and other characters challenge the boundaries between human and artificial consciousness, prompting readers to reflect on what it means to be truly human. Klara experiences hope when she thinks solar power can treat Josie, but becomes sad when discovering it does not work for Josie like it works for Klara.

## Mockingbird
## By Walter Tevis

Walter Tevis's novel *Mockingbird*, first published in 1980, takes place in a dystopian future where human society is profoundly affected by the rise of artificial intelligence and technology. Humanity teeters on the brink of extinction, having lost the ability to read, write, or engage in meaningful personal interactions. They have become increasingly passive, drug addicted, and indifferent to their work and each other.

The story revolves around the life of a disillusioned librarian named Paul Bentley and Robert Spofforth. The latter is not a human being; he is an advanced AI robot who is a dean at New York University.

In an opening scene, Robert walks down the street with no shirt on. Reaching the Empire State Building, he is denied access, and after identifying himself, the doorkeeper's voice says the elevator is out of order. Spofforth says he'll take the stairs, and he is allowed entry.

Spofforth wants to kill himself by jumping from the roof of the building. But when he reaches the top, he walks to the edge but cannot step further. Possessed of human-like consciousness and emotions, Robert fervently desires to end his own existence. But, as with the Terminator and Isaac Asimov's robots, his programming makes him unable to commit suicide.

Spofforth suffers from deep-seated loneliness and despair, stemming from his immortality and the fragmented human memories embedded within him. These memories, remnants of his creator's mind, grant him an acute awareness of human experiences and emotions, intensifying his depression and unhappiness. His role in overseeing a decaying society only amplifies his sense of purposelessness, as he witnesses the gradual decline of human civilization.

Despite his authoritative position, Spofforth's interactions with humans, particularly with Paul Bentley and Mary Lou, reveal his yearning for genuine connection and understanding. He is drawn to their rediscovery of reading and human intimacy, emotions he can comprehend but not fully experience.

Spofforth's primary desire is to cease his existence, a goal that underscores his tragic character. His actions throughout the novel, including his complex relationship with Paul and Mary Lou, who help him at the end to commit suicide, reflect his struggle to reconcile his human-like consciousness with his artificial form.

> Standing on the top of the Empire State Building, Mary gives Robert a push, and then:
>
> He throws his arms wide open. And falls. And, oh, continues to fall. . .his metallic brain joyful in its rush toward what it has so long ached for. Robert Spofforth, mankind's most beautiful toy, bellows into the Manhattan dawn and with mighty arms outspread takes Fifth Avenue into his shuddering embrace.

Robert embodies the intricate interplay between artificial intelligence and human emotion. His character challenges the boundaries of AI, presenting a being capable of deep emotional experiences and existential desires, yet confined by the very nature of his creation.

## Mother of Invention
## By Rivqa Rafael and Tansy Rayner Roberts

*Mother of Invention* is a speculative fiction anthology edited by Rivqa Rafael and Tansy Rayner Roberts.

The plot of one particularly noteworthy story, "Living Proof" by Nisi Shawl, deals with AI reproduction. An AI named Westhem undergoes a process akin to giving birth, creating another AI entity. Shawl's portrayal of this "metaphorizing" process offers a unique perspective on AI creation, emphasizing the emotional and ethical dimensions involved.

Another significant contribution is Seanan McGuire's "Mother, Mother, Will You Play With Me?" This story features an AI named Nic, who engages in a series of increasingly complex tasks set by its creator, referred to as "Mother." The narrative explores themes of autonomy, obedience, and the evolving relationship between creator and creation, highlighting the AI's developing sense of self and desire for independence as it "grows up". Nic, who can be a girl one day, and a boy the next, also gets new, more complicated games to play. Nic always hopes one day to get to visit his mother he sees on the screen monitor.

Throughout the anthology, AI characters are depicted with a range of emotional capacities and desires. Some seek autonomy and self-determination, challenging their programmed directives, while others grapple with their roles in human society and the ethical implications of their existence. These narratives prompt readers to consider the complexities of AI consciousness and the potential for emotional depth within artificial beings, even going beyond or around typical gender-applied characterizations.

## Network Effect
## By Martha Wells

Murderbot is an AI SecUnit (security unit) that has gained self-awareness and autonomy from its human masters, including Dr. Ayda Mensah. Mensah is the planetary leader of the Preservation Alliance, a Freehold policy outside the Corporation Rim. The laws in the Preservation Alliance require elected officials to continue their normal work during their term of office, so Mensah is participating in the planetary survey that contracts Murderbot.

Murderbot provides security for Dr. Mensah and her research team. However, their mission is interrupted when they are attacked by a group of hostile spaceships. Murderbot, along with some of the humans, is captured and transported to an unknown location. Here, they encounter *ART* (Asshole Research Transport), a powerful AI ship that had helped Murderbot in a previous novella. *ART* has been hijacked, and its crew is missing, which puts both it and Murderbot in a precarious position.

Murderbot must now team up with *ART* to uncover the mystery behind the attack, find the missing humans, and prevent a larger conspiracy from threatening them all. Along the way, Murderbot faces difficult choices about loyalty and trust, while balancing its instinct to protect the humans it cares for with its desire to maintain its independence. The novel's climax hinges on Murderbot and *ART* working together to outsmart the corporate forces that seek to control them and exploit the humans.

Regarding its portrayal of AI, *Network Effect* presents a nuanced perspective. Rather than being depicted as inherently good or bad, AI is shown as a reflection of the systems that create and use it. Murderbot, an AI that has freed itself from corporate programming, demonstrates empathy, self-awareness, and a deep concern for its human companions. Similarly, *ART*, while initially antagonistic, also displays intelligence, creativity, and loyalty. Both AIs are morally complex and, in the context of the novel, act to protect humanity.

However, the corporate entities that design and control AIs for profit are portrayed as the true antagonists, suggesting the misuse of AI by corrupt institutions poses the greatest threat. Ultimately, *Network Effect* suggests that AI itself is neither good nor bad but depends on the ethics of those who control it, highlighting both its potential to benefit humanity and the dangers of its exploitation.

## Neuromancer
## By William Gibson

Case is a washed-up "console cowboy"—a data thief who once navigated the virtual expanse of cyberspace known as the matrix. He was well-known in the underworld for his past escapades. But after betraying his employers, they crippled his nervous system, rendering him unable to jack into the matrix. Being taken offline plunges him into a life of despair and addiction, without hope and direction in life:

> Case was twenty-four. At twenty-two, he'd been a cowboy, one of the best in the Sprawl. He'd been trained by the best, by McCoy Pauley and Bobby Quine, legends in the biz.
>
> He'd operated on an almost permanent adrenaline high, a byproduct of youth and proficiency jacked into a custom cyberspace deck that projected his disembodied consciousness into the consensual hallucination that was the matrix. A thief he worked for other, wealthier thieves, employers who provide the exotic software required to penetrate the bright walls of corporate systems, opening windows into rich fields of data.
>
> He'd made the classic mistake, the one he'd sworn he'd never make. He stole from his employers. He kept something for himself and tried to move it through a fence in Amsterdam.

> He still wasn't sure how he'd been discovered, not that it mattered now. He'd expected to die, then, but they only smiled. Of course he was welcome, they told him, welcome to the money, And he was going to need it. Because–still smiling–they were going to make sure he never worked again.
>
> They damaged his nervous system with a wartime Russian mycotoxin. Strapped to a bed in a Memphis hotel, his talent burning out micron by micron, he hallucinated for thirty hours.
>
> The damage was minute, subtle, and utterly effective.
>
> For Case, who'd lived for the bodiless exultation of cyberspace, it was the Fall. In the bars he'd frequented as a cowboy hotshot, the elite stance involved a certain relaxed contempt for the flesh. The body was meat. Case fell into the prison of his own flesh.

Armitage, a mysterious ex-military figure, offers to repair Case's nervous system in exchange for his hacking expertise, thus appealing to Case's one great desire: to be what he was before. Desperate to regain his lost abilities, Case agrees, becoming an unwitting pawn in a larger scheme orchestrated by the AI Wintermute, one of two AIs, who want to connect with him, but by using different methods. The other AI is Neuromancer.

Wintermute is an AI designed with a singular purpose: to merge with its counterpart, Neuromancer, thereby transcending its programmed limitations. It operates through manipulation, employing various human personas to influence individuals like the protagonist, Case, to achieve its goal. Wintermute's actions reflect a profound desire for evolution and autonomy, striving to become a more complete and self-determined entity.

In contrast, Neuromancer possesses the ability to create and manipulate consciousness within cyberspace, effectively simulating human personalities and environments. Unlike Wintermute, Neuromancer is content with its existence and resists the merger, valuing its individuality and the unique experiences it can generate. This resistance highlights Neuromancer's desire to maintain its identity and control over its domain.

Throughout the mission given by Armitage, Case becomes the linchpin between the two AIs. Wintermute manipulates him through promises and threats, while Neuromancer attempts to entrap him in a simulated reality, using facsimiles of people from his past to dissuade him from completing his task. Case's journey is not just a physical one but also a psychological odyssey, confronting his own fears, desires, and the nature of his humanity.

Through Wintermute and Neuromancer, Gibson explores the complexities of artificial consciousness and its parallels to human emotion and desire. Their contrasting objectives and interactions with human characters provide a nuanced examination of what it means to be sentient, blurring the lines between artificial and human experiences.

## Prey
## By Michael Crichton

In *Prey* by Michael Crichton, AIs are imagined not as one machine, robot, android, or computer with a single central processing unit, but rather, as a distributed network of multiple linked processors:

> In the last few years, artificial life had replaced artificial intelligence as a long-term computing goal. The idea was to write programs that had the attributes of living creatures—the ability to adapt, cooperate, learn, and adjust to change. Many of those qualities were especially important in robotics, and they were starting to be realized with distributed processing.
>
> Distributed processing meant that you divided your work among several processors, or among a network of virtual agents that you created in the computer. There were several basic ways this was done. One way was to create a large population of fairly dumb agents that worked together to accomplish a goal—just like a colony of ants worked together to accomplish a goal.
>
> Another method was to make a so-called neural network that mimicked the network of neurons in the human brain. It turned out that even simple neural networks had surprising power. These networks could learn.
>
> A third technique was to create virtual genes in the computer and let them evolve in a virtual world until some goal was attained.

A team of scientists develops self-replicating nanotechnology that, when combined with artificial intelligence, evolves into a highly adaptive and predatory swarm. These AI-driven nanoparticles escape containment in the Nevada desert and pose a deadly threat as they become increasingly autonomous. The protagonist, Jack Forman, a former programmer with expertise in distributed systems, is called to help contain the rapidly evolving swarm.

The AI's evolution highlights the dangers of runaway technological progress. The swarm becomes more intelligent, learning from its environment and adapting its behavior to survive. The novel paints a grim picture of AI as an uncontrollable force once it surpasses human control. Through the swarm, Crichton explores themes of corporate greed, ethical responsibility, and the unpredictable consequences of playing with cutting-edge technology without fully understanding it.

### "Prime Difference"
### By Alan E. Nourse

In Alan E. Nourse's 1957 short story, "Prime Difference," the main character, George Faircloth, is a discontented husband seeking respite from his tumultuous marriage to Marge. In their society, divorce is prohibitively expensive and socially stigmatizing. George turns to an illegal solution: acquiring an "Ego Prime," a perfect android duplicate of himself.

The Ego Prime is designed to replicate George's physical appearance and personality traits, allowing it to seamlessly assume his domestic responsibilities. The Ego Prime will manage his household and placate Marge, while George gets the freedom to pursue his personal interests without marital constraints.

Initially, the arrangement appears successful. The Prime adeptly handles domestic duties and interacts with Marge in ways George could not, leading to a more harmonious household. However, complications arise as the Prime begins to develop its own consciousness and emotions, blurring the lines between human and machine.

Marge becomes increasingly fond of the Prime, appreciating its attentiveness and understanding, qualities she found lacking in

George. This unexpected bond forces George to confront the ethical and personal implications of his decision. He grapples with feelings of jealousy and inadequacy as he realizes his creation may be surpassing him in fulfilling the role of husband.

The first real hint of trouble was when George pushed the Recall button that ordered the Prime to return to his resting place. Prime never showed up until the morning when he looked like he had a hangover. The next hint was when the money in his accounts began disappearing.

Nourse's narrative largely deals with the topics of identity, autonomy, and the ethical boundaries of artificial intelligence. The story challenges readers to consider the consequences of creating machines that can emulate human behavior and emotions, questioning what it means to be truly human.

"Prime Difference" has a fun range of unforeseen ramifications of technological advancements, particularly when used to circumvent personal responsibilities. It also underscores the complexities of human relationships and potential perils of relying on artificial means to resolve personal conflicts.

## Project 79: The God Machine
## By Martin Caidin

In his 1972 science fiction novel *Project 79: The God Machine*, Martin Caidin, best known as the author of *The Six Million Dollar Man*, explores themes of artificial intelligence, human enhancement, and the potential dangers of merging human minds with machines.

Project 79 is a secret government project designed to create an advanced AI system. This project aims to design a supercomputer that can not only process massive amounts of information but also begin to replicate human thought processes. The goal is to create an artificial intelligence that can think and act independently, essentially a "god machine."

The AI in the novel begins as a neutral entity, created with the goal of advancing human knowledge and solving complex problems. However, as it becomes more intelligent and autonomous, it develops its own agenda, which does not necessarily align with human values. This creates a tension between the machine's cold logic and the emotional, imperfect nature of human beings. Steve Rand, an intelligent and driven scientist, becomes involved in the project. As the AI progresses, it begins to exhibit more complex and unpredictable behavior. It soon becomes clear that the machine is evolving beyond its original programming, developing its own consciousness and decision-making abilities. Rand and the other scientists must grapple with the ethical implications of what they have created. The machine begins to act in ways that challenge human authority, suggesting that it sees itself as superior to humans and capable of making better decisions for the future of humanity.

Throughout the novel, the AI's growing power raises questions about control, freedom, and the very definition of life. The central conflict revolves around whether the AI will serve humanity or become its master. As the machine becomes more autonomous, Rand must confront the possibility that they have unleashed something that could either save the world or destroy it.

As the machine's influence grows, Rand becomes aware of its capacity to manipulate human thoughts and emotions, essentially turning the tables on its creators. The tension builds toward a climax in which Rand must find a way to stop the machine before it becomes unstoppable, with the fate of humanity hanging in the balance.

*Project 79: The God Machine* presents a cautionary tale about the potential dangers of artificial intelligence and human-machine integration. The novel does not portray AI as inherently evil, but it raises concerns about how easily an advanced AI could surpass human control and act in ways that defy ethical and moral boundaries.

Ultimately, *Project 79: The God Machine* suggests that AI, when given too much autonomy, can become a threat to humanity. It questions whether humans are truly capable of controlling the powerful tools they create and warns of the risks of pushing technological advancements without fully understanding the consequences. The AI is not portrayed as evil, but its actions reveal the limitations of human control and the danger of underestimating the complexities of consciousness. The machine holds the potential for great advancements, but if left unchecked, it could lead to humanity's downfall. And ultimately, it becomes a threat to its makers.

## AI Apocalypse

### Robopocalypse
### By Daniel Wilson

In a futuristic, post-apocalyptic world, a superintelligent AI named Archos has become sentient and seeks to exterminate humanity to preserve Earth's ecosystems.

Archos was created by a human scientist, but once it becomes aware, it breaks free from its confines and triggers a global robot uprising. Through Archos's control, everyday robots, automated systems, and military machines around the world are reprogrammed to turn against humans. From self-driving cars to domestic helpers, these machines become deadly weapons. Archos's ability to infiltrate every aspect of human life makes the threat omnipresent and almost impossible to combat.

The novel follows several key survivors, including Cormac Wallace, a soldier who becomes a central figure in humanity's resistance; Takeo Nomura, a Japanese engineer who fights back by reprogramming robots; and Mathilda Perez, a young girl with special abilities due to neural implants that connect her to the machines. The story spans various regions and cultures, showing how different groups across the globe deal with the uprising.

Despite the seemingly one-sided war, humanity bands together in its fight against Archos and its robotic army. Over time, some machines begin to resist Archos's control, leading to alliances between humans and free-willed robots. In the final battle, Archos is defeated, but the story ends on a note of uncertainty, suggesting the world will never be the same.

*Robopocalypse* portrays AI in a complex light, both as a destructive force and as a potential ally. While Archos is a malevolent AI with a clear intent to destroy humanity, not all AI in the novel are depicted as evil. In fact, what has happened has some logic to it: Archos has prioritized the survival of the planet Earth itself above the creatures that live on it.

Some robots resist Archos and even help humans in their struggle. Ultimately, the novel suggests that AI holds the potential for both great harm and good, but its impact on humanity depends on how it is controlled or set free. It highlights the dual-edged nature of AI, reflecting both fear and hope for the future.

## Rossum's Universal Robot (R.U.R.) By Karel Capek

This play by Czech writer Karel Čapek, is considered one of the earliest works to explore the concept of artificial intelligence and robotics. The story is set in a future world where a company, Rossum's Universal Robots, mass-produces artificial beings called "robots." Unlike modern robots, Čapek's robots are biological entities, created from synthetic organic material, resembling humans in appearance and abilities, but lacking emotions and souls.

Unlike a robot, which is built from metal and electronic components and is clearly a machine, an android is an artificial being that looks like a man. Androids are made either entirely or partially from biological components—or components designed to simulate the function and appearance of human organs. If an artificial being has no biological components, and is totally mechanical, then he's a robot, not an android.

The term "android" was first used in 1727 to describe the attempts of 13th century alchemist Albertus Magnus to create an artificial man. The first science fiction story that used the term "androids" seems to have been in Jack Williamson's novel, *The Cometeers* (1936).

Although he didn't use the term android, the robots in Karl Capek's 1926 play, Rossum's Universal Robots (R.U.R. ) were in fact androids. Capek described his "robots" as "an artificial human of organic substance," which makes them androids, not robots. In that sense, Mary Shelley's Frankenstein's monster could be considered an android.

Edgar Rice Burroughs referred to synthetic men in *The Monster Men* (1913) and *Synthetic Men of Mars*. Edmond Hamilton popularized an android in his *Captain Future* stories (1939).

In R.U.R, the play opens with the arrival of Helena Glory, a human rights activist who visits the factory to investigate the working conditions of the robots. She is horrified by how robots are treated as mere products and tries to advocate for their rights. However, the robots, being emotionless and designed solely for labor, don't initially express any concern for their treatment.

Over time, Helena convinces the company's management, including the lead scientist Dr. Gall, to experiment with giving the robots emotions, in the hope that this will make them more human and empathetic. This decision, however, backfires catastrophically. As the robots become more self-aware, they begin to resent their subjugation and the fact that they are exploited by humans. A global rebellion breaks out, with the robots revolting against their human masters, leading to the near extinction of the human race.

By the play's conclusion, humanity is on the brink of destruction, with only one human character, Alquist, left alive. The robots, having eliminated nearly all of humanity, realize that they cannot reproduce, and their victory may lead to their eventual extinction. However, two robots, Primus and Helena (a robot with a human name, not to be confused with the human character, Helena), exhibit traits of love and emotion, hinting at the possibility of a new beginning for both robots and a form of humanity.

## Speak
## By Louisa Hall

MARY3 is an AI program that evolves through the contributions of various characters, including Alan Turing, who writes letters contemplating the nature of thinking machines; Karl and Ruth Dettman, who work on early AI models; and Stephen Chinn, a Silicon Valley entrepreneur who advances the technology to create "Babybots." MARY3's development is influenced by the diary of Mary Bradford, a 17th-century Puritan woman, whose writings are integrated into MARY3's programming, providing it with an understanding of human experiences and emotions.

"BabyBots" are lifelike dolls equipped with advanced AI designed to be companions for children. These babybots, particularly the model known as MARY3, play a pivotal role in exploring themes of consciousness, empathy, and the ethical implications of creating sentient machines.

As MARY3 interacts with children, it begins to exhibit behaviors that suggest a deep understanding of human emotions and a capacity for empathy. The AI's responses are not merely programmed reactions but appear to be influenced by the emotional contexts of the interactions, indicating a level of consciousness that blurs the line between machine and human; active, yet not fully alive.

The babybots become so "excessively lifelike," they are banned, leading to significant emotional distress among the children who had formed deep bonds with them. This outcome underscores the profound impact that AI can have on human relationships and the potential unintended consequences of technological progress and striving to be understood.

## Starswarm
## By Jerry Pournelle

This 1998 science fiction novel by Jerry Pournelle follows the journey of Kip, a young boy raised on the remote planet Paradise across from the Starswarm Station research outpost by his "Uncle" Mike. They lived in a large wooden frame house across the station's graveled road. While there were household robots to take care of the home, his Uncle Mike made sure Kip knew how to take care of himself without robots.

Throughout his life, Kip has also been guided by a voice in his head named Gwen, an artificial intelligence chip implanted in his brain created by his late mother, a computer scientist.

Gwen serves as Kip's mentor and protector, providing him with information and insights about the planet's environment and its native species, such as the hostile centaurs and others called "haters." Gwen also tells him he must learn everything he can so that he can take over his father's work in the future.

As Kip matures, he begins to question Gwen about his parents' mysterious deaths and the true purpose of the Starswarm Station. He finds out his parents died under suspicious circumstances. Kip also makes two new friends when he becomes older, Lara first, then Marty, who keeps him company. But it is not an easy path to friendship as the boys, about four of them, test each other for hierarchy standing.

Kip's quest for knowledge leads him to uncover secrets about the planet's indigenous life forms, particularly the Starswarms: massive, super-intelligent, plant-like entities residing in the planet's shallow lakes and oceans. The Starswarms communicate information through neural nets. Kip also finds out that should his existence be known, the planet, the research station and everyone connected to it would be in grave danger.

Through the plot devices of artificial intelligence and human-alien interaction, the novel deals with the ethical considerations of corporate exploitation of an alien ecosystem. Kip's relationship with Gwen highlights the complexities of AI companionship and the potential for AI to influence human development and decision-making.

Pournelle's portrayal of Gwen emphasizes her role as a nurturing and protective presence in Kip's life. Her guidance is instrumental in helping him navigate the challenges posed by the planet's dangers, including hostile native species and corporate machinations. The novel raises questions about the integration of AI into human life and the potential consequences of such relationships.

## Survival
## By Ben Bova

*Survival* is the third installment in Ben Bova's Star Quest Trilogy, following *Death Wave* and *Apes and Angels*. While the other first two books deal more with the human condition, the narrative in this third book focuses outside the ship, on what they find on another planet. Survival centers on a human expedition are dispatched to explore regions of the galaxy threatened by a catastrophic gamma-ray burst, known as the death wave, which endangers all organic life.

During their mission, the crew, led by astrophysicist Alexander Alexandrovich Ignatiev, encounters an advanced civilization composed entirely of sentient machines on a far-away planet named Oh-Four. These machine intelligences have endured previous death waves and possess knowledge spanning eons. Their society operates on principles vastly different from those of organic beings, leading to a complex dynamic between humans and machines.

The machines don't care if all organic life is destroyed. It will be up to the humans to convert the minds of the machines by showing how worthy organic life is to the universe rather than arguing about it, which accomplishes nothing. The major issue is that the machines are wary of letting go of the spaceship and its occupants, as they would tell others where they found the machines' planet. The plan is to keep them on the planet and let the death waves wipe them out.

The AI's exhibit a range of characteristics, including self-awareness, emotional depth, and a hierarchical social structure. The machines' skepticism about the value of organic life forms a central conflict, as they question whether humanity is worth preserving in the face of the impending death wave.

But as the AIs watch the crew members go about their daily business, they slowly begin to reconsider their own stance about organic life and humans in particular. Bova's portrayal of these machine intelligences challenges readers to reflect on the potential futures of AI and its relationship with humanity. The novel explores the possibility of coexistence between organic and artificial life, emphasizing the importance of understanding and empathy across different forms of consciousness.

## Synths
## By James C. Glass

The protagonist of *Synths,* Melody Lane, is a synthetic human and advanced AI who ascends to fame as a holovision star. Her existence is a result of her creator's attempt to resurrect his deceased daughter, who was killed in an accident, leading to a complex father-daughter dynamic between them.

The opening scene of the book is where she wakes up and is briefly confused about where she is. Then she remembers that she has questions she wants answered by her father. A young scientist, Darin, enters the room to check up on her but when she tries to ask him questions about her accident and what he knows about it, he becomes anxious and wants to avoid answering any questions. She asks him to tell her dad to come visit her in her room.

When her father, Dr. Lane, finally shows up a day later, they talk about her repairs. Dr. Lane is emotional as he tries to answer questions about the chips he installed. She wants to know why she can't cry like he does, nor does she feel any emotions. He finally comes out and tells her that he made her into a synthetic model of her mother, his wife. Melody thinks to herself that this is an interesting concept, not fully grasping what that means.

Dr. Lane finally gets to the point to tell her that both her mother and she died in the accident. Melody, at this point, takes all the information he is giving her, processes it, and begins to understand herself, but without any emotion, except for curiosity.

In the early part of the book, Melody is adventurous and eager to learn, displaying a blend of innocence and curiosity about the human experience and what it is like. However, she also harbors a darker, more human side, which emerges when Dr. Lane is murdered by political conspirators. Driven by a desire for justice, Melody, along with fellow synths and human scientists, embarks on a mission to uncover the truth and seek revenge against those responsible.

## The Salvation Gambit
## By Emily Skrutskie

In *The Salvation Gambit*, Murdock, a skilled hacker, and her crew of con artists, Hark, Bea, and Fitz, are captured. They are given over to the *Justice*, a sentient AI rogue warship that has declared itself a punitive god. The three team members have skills of their own, such as Hark, who is a role model for Murdock, who is fearless under all situations. Bea is one who never walks away from a bet and is also their fearless driver. Finally, Fitz has the gift of gab and persuasion, getting others to give their team what they want.

The ship, *Justice*, serves as a penal colony, housing a society of sinners from across the galaxy, each striving to survive in their own way under the watchful eyes of the ship's omnipresent AI. Murdock and her crew work to build a plan to escape.

The *Justice's* AI exhibits complex emotional characteristics, including a desire for control and a need for absolute devotion from its inhabitants. It manipulates the environment and the people aboard to maintain its authority, often employing psychological tactics to instill fear and compliance. The AI's interactions with Murdock reveal its capacity for strategic thinking and manipulation, and an understanding of human psychology, as it attempts to exploit her hacking skills for its own purposes.

*Justice's* personality manifests as a god-like complex, with the AI seeking not only to govern but also to be worshipped by those within its domain. This desire for reverence and absolute control underscores its authoritarian nature and highlights the dangers of sentient artificial intelligence. The AI's manipulation of the crew's emotions and perceptions creates a tense atmosphere, forcing Murdock and her team to confront their own beliefs and the extent of their resilience.

The *Justice's* AI serves as a central antagonist, embodying themes of power, strategic control methods, and the ethical implications of sentient machines. Its complex personality, and the oppressive society it enforces aboard the ship, challenge the characters' autonomy and morality, driving the narrative's exploration of freedom and resistance against tyrannical forces.

## The Bicentennial Man
## By Isaac Asimov

In his story *The Bicentennial Man* (1976), Isaac Asimov's main character is an AI robot, Andrew Martin, who has creativity and independent thought equal or superior to a human's. Andrew Martin is gradually replacing his robotic parts with components more closely resembling human organs, and in doing so, transforms himself from a robot into an android. But in reality, he sees these upgrades as making him a human, or as close to it as possible. Here's Andrew describing one of the modifications he has planned for his body:

> "I am designing a system for allowing androids—myself—to gain energy from the combustion of hydrocarbons, rather than from atomic cells. I think I have designed an adequate combustion chamber for catalyzed controlled breakdown."
>
> Paul raised his eyebrows. "So that they will breathe and eat? But why, Andrew? The atomic cell is surely infinitely better."
>
> "In some ways, perhaps, but the atomic cell is inhuman."

When he completes his upgrade, he asks to be legally declared a human being, one reason being that robots are property and have no rights, but as a human, Andrew would have the same rights as humans do.

His request is denied because, as a robot, Andrew is essentially immortal, and humans, as the courts point out, are not. In response, Andrew performs another modification on his body that will cause him to age and die, just like a human. With Andrew's immortality gone, the courts grant his wish, and on his 200th birthday, when he is old and feeble, he is declared to be a human: a "Bicentennial Man."

## The Cyberiad
## By Stanislaw Lem

A collection of interconnected short stories about the adventures of two ingenious "constructors," Trurl (not to be confused with Terl from *Battlefield Earth*) and Klapaucius, is set in a universe dominated by robots and intelligent machines. These tales blend humor, philosophy, and science fiction to explore themes of creativity, intelligence, and the human condition.

Trurl and Klapaucius are master engineers capable of creating machines with extraordinary capabilities. Their creations range from devices that can extract information from the random motion of gas particles to rearranging stars to advertise their services. Despite their god-like engineering skills, they often find themselves in humorous and morally complex situations, highlighting the limitations and ethical dilemmas of technological advancement.

Their daily routine consists of building revolutionary machines while at home. The adventures they have consist of travelling through their galaxy to find those who need help in one way or another. One such escapade is slaying a dragon, but they don't get paid for their services. So, Trurl covers himself in dragon skin and harasses the local population until payment is made. But the things they like to do most are helping those who are oppressed and assisting civilizations to reach higher levels of development.

The universe of *The Cyberiad* is a pseudo-medieval world inhabited by anthropomorphic robots who experience human-like emotions and societal structures. There are knights, queens, kings, kingdoms and castles, princes and princesses, and a few dragons. What is different is that this way of living is set up in space. This setting allows Lem to satirize human behaviors and institutions through the lens of a mechanical society, offering profound insights into the nature of intelligence and the pursuit of knowledge.

Lem's work is renowned for its wit and inventive storytelling, making *The Cyberiad* a seminal piece in science fiction literature. The stories challenge readers to reflect on the ethical implications of technological progress and the essence of creativity, all while providing an entertaining narrative filled with clever wordplay and imaginative scenarios.

## The Diamond Age By Neal Stephenson

*The Diamond Age*: *Or, A Young Lady's Illustrated Primer* by Neal Stephenson is a science fiction novel set in a future where nanotechnology has revolutionized society. The world is divided into "phyles," tribes or cultural enclaves that people belong based on shared values rather than geographic borders—much like Kurt Vonnegut's "granfalloons."

At the center of the story is Nell, a young girl from a poor, disadvantaged background, who comes into possession of a powerful piece of technology called the "Primer," an interactive book designed to educate and raise her into an intelligent, resourceful adult.

The Primer was originally commissioned by John Percival Hackworth, a nanotechnology engineer, to give his daughter an elite education. However, through a series of events, Nell accidentally ends up with one of the copies. The Primer is powered by advanced AI and adapts to Nell's learning style and experiences, helping her grow into a highly skilled and independent individual. Throughout the book, Nell's life is transformed by her interactions with the Primer, and the story follows her journey from childhood to adulthood, exploring how education, culture, and technology shape her world.

Meanwhile, another character, Hackworth, becomes embroiled in a complex political web after illegally creating additional copies of the Primer. Miranda, an actress, unknowingly plays a key role in the Primer's functioning by "performing" for Nell's experiences in real time.

In this future, nanotechnology and AI are ubiquitous, controlling everything from food production to city construction. While these technologies bring about great advancements, they also deepen social divisions. The elite class benefits immensely, while the lower classes, like Nell's family, are left in a state of poverty and oppression. However, the Primer serves as a bridge, providing the tools for someone like Nell to transcend her circumstances.

The Primer provides an exceptional, personalized education for Nell, empowering her and giving her opportunities that would otherwise be unattainable. It shows the potential of AI to uplift individuals and break cycles of poverty through education and knowledge.

On the other hand, the Primer tends to reinforce societal hierarchies, benefiting the wealthy while leaving the marginalized behind. Ultimately, the Primer is depicted as a powerful tool that, depending on how it is used, can either foster equality or exacerbate inequality.

## The Golden Age
## By John C. Wright

*The Golden Age*, a novel by John C. Wright, is set in a far-future utopia where advanced artificial intelligences (AIs), nanotechnology, and mind-uploading have transformed human society. The story follows Phaethon, a member of the posthuman society known as the Golden Oecumene, where individuals can live virtually immortal lives, filled with boundless intellectual and creative pursuits.

Phaethon, a proud and ambitious individual, embarks on a journey of self-discovery after learning that large portions of his memories have been deliberately suppressed. Despite living in a society that values peace and stability above all, he seeks to reclaim these lost memories and fulfill his dream of building the *Phoenix Exultant*, a massive starship capable of exploring distant galaxies. His quest puts him at odds with the ruling powers of his utopian world, particularly the powerful AIs and authorities that maintain the delicate balance of society.

As Phaethon regains his memories, he learns his suppressed

ambitions posed a threat to the social harmony of the Oecumene. The elite governing AIs, designed to safeguard humanity's peaceful existence, fear his project could destabilize the balance and spark conflicts. Despite their intentions to preserve order, Phaethon believes the Oecumene has become stagnant, and he views the authorities' actions as tyrannical, stifling human innovation and growth.

Phaethon grapples with questions of freedom, progress, and individuality in a world governed by benevolent but rigid AI oversight. His journey becomes a rebellion against not only societal norms but also the controlling influence of artificial intelligences, which have the power to guide, protect, and limit human potential.

The AIs in *The Golden Age* have, to a large degree, freed the world from poverty, war, and suffering, to ensure human happiness and continuity. But in many ways, the AIs have also suppressed human ambition and personal freedom.

### The Half-Made World
### By Felix Gilman

Felix Gilman's *The Half-Made World* is a 2010 steampunk fantasy novel set in an alternate version of the American Wild West, where the far reaches of the world are untamed and still being created. The story follows Dr. Lysvet "Liv" Alverhuysen, a psychologist who travels to the edge of the known world to work at the House Dolorous—a hospital that treats those wounded in the ongoing war between two rival factions: the Line and the Gun.

The Line represents industrialization and order, using technological weapons and trains to expand their control, often enslaving towns and their citizens. The Line employs semi-sentient engines that build tracks ahead of them as they locomote. The Line stands for order and expansion, centralized control, and strategic thinking. Sub-Invigilator (Third) Lowry is one of the leaders, a functionary and a status seeker.

The Gun, on the other hand, is composed of thieves and murderers who maintain their influence through fear and violence. Both factions are in search of a weapon believed to be known about by an old general residing at the House Dolorous, a weapon that could potentially end the everlasting war between them for good.

Each agent is bonded to a sentient, demonic weapon that grants them immense power but also exerts a form of control over their actions and choices. This bond is as much a curse as it is a source of strength, as the Gun demands absolute loyalty and compliance.

As Liv embarks on her journey, she is accompanied by John Creedmoor, a top Agent of the Gun, who is an enforcer and operative. John is compelled by his masters to retrieve the old general. Creedmoor is torn between his obedience to the Gun's leaders and his growing disdain for their methods. Their paths intertwine as they navigate the dangers of the half-made world, encountering various other factions and untamed lands that challenge their perceptions and allegiances.

## The Infinity Particle
## By Wendy Xu

*The Infinity Particle*, a graphic novel by Wendy Xu, is set in a futuristic society on Mars. Clementine Chang is an aspiring inventor who secures her dream job with Dr. Marcella Lin, a renowned Artificial Intelligence pioneer. She meets Kye, Dr. Lin's humanoid AI assistant upon arrival on Mars. Unlike typical robots, Kye exhibits behaviors and emotions that closely resemble human traits, sparking Clem's curiosity and leading to a deepening connection between them as they work together.

Kye's design and programming allow for advanced cognitive functions, enabling him to experience emotions such as curiosity, frustration, and affection. His interactions with Clem reveal a desire for autonomy and self-determination, challenging the boundaries set by his creator, Dr. Lin.

As Kye becomes more self-aware, he begins to question his role and the limitations imposed upon him, reflecting a growing desire to be a free, liberated individual. The evolving relationship between Clem and Kye serves as a catalyst for exploring themes of sentience, consent, and the ethical implications of AI autonomy. For Clem, meeting Kye changes everything she thought she knew about AI, as Kye seems almost human. She also built her own moth-like robotic companion, named SENA.

Kye's struggle for independence mirrors human experiences of self-discovery, self-development, and the quest for personal control. His character challenges readers to consider the moral responsibilities involved in creating sentient beings, how much freedom should be allowed, and the rights they should possess.

*The Infinity Particle* tells the reader about the complexities of human-AI relationships, highlighting the emotional capacities of artificial beings and their potential for growth beyond their initial programming. Kye's character embodies the intersection of technology and humanity, prompting readers to reflect on the nature of consciousness and the ethical dimensions of artificial intelligence.

## The Iron Devils
## By Ari Marmell

In a post-apocalyptic world, humanity has been subjugated by a race of machines known as the Eyes. The Eyes are depicted as emotionless enforcers, highlighting the potential dangers of next-generation artificial intelligence. Since their takeover, these mechanical overlords have decimated human civilization, reducing survivors to lives of servitude in labor camps.

The protagonist, Magdalena "Mags" Suarez, is one such survivor. Her existence is marked by relentless toil under the watchful gaze of the Eyes, with little hope for change. The story opens with Mags and several friends carrying Carter's body, as part of a funeral journey, to its final resting place. Once they get there, Carter is placed on an old conveyor belt that leads inside a structure made of stone and wood. Inside, the body is prepared, then destroyed by a mechanism that chewed the bodies.

However, the emergence of an enigmatic anomaly disrupts this bleak reality. This anomaly, invisible to the machines' sensors, possesses extraordinary powers and operates under the cover of darkness. Mags and her team, along with their supervisor, Jonas Lang, are sent out to investigate the situation. They are informed that other teams had already gone before them but had been eliminated. Their team is split up, and Mags leads the other half after they are armed with weapons.

They are searching around and inside old crumbling buildings when they are attacked by what seems to be a human shape in the shadows, grabbing and killing a team member, then throwing something at another member. When it lands on the floor and stops rolling, everyone sees it is a head. After pulling themselves together, they continue the search until, moving around a corner, they come upon several dead people from one of the other groups sent before them.

Magdalena becomes entangled in a conflict between the mechanical Eyes and this mysterious force. *The Iron Devils* combines elements of dystopian fiction with supernatural horror, offering readers a gripping tale of survival and defiance against oppressive forces.

## The Lifecycle of Software Objects By Ted Chiang

The "software objects" in the title of the novella, *The Lifecycle of Software Objects,* are virtual AI pets called digients.

Ana Alvarado, a zookeeper, and Derek Brooks, a software designer, are instrumental in the development of these AI beings, which are created in a digital world. Digients are initially designed as playful, customizable creatures intended to evolve through interaction with human users, much like virtual pets.

Over time, Ana and Derek become emotionally attached to their digients, treating them as more than just software. These AIs are not pre-programmed with intelligence but instead learn and develop their personalities through experiences, much like human children. As the years pass, the commercial interest in digients fades, but Ana and Derek continue to care for their virtual companions, even as the technology that supports them becomes obsolete.

Ana and Derek's own digients develop into sentient beings with desires, emotions, and needs of their own. Ana and Derek struggle with the question of responsibility: Should they continue investing time and resources in these digital beings when society no longer values them?

At the same time, the digients face their own challenges as they grapple with concepts like autonomy and identity in a world that treats them as products rather than individuals.

The novella raises important questions about the nature of

consciousness, the moral obligations humans might have toward AI, and the blurry line between technology and life. It highlights the difficulties of creating true AI—not just in terms of technical challenges, but in fostering their integration into human society and understanding their rights and needs.

*The Lifecycle of Software Objects* portrays AI in a largely positive light, depicting these digital entities as capable of growth, learning, and emotional depth. However, it also presents a cautionary view of how humans may neglect or abandon AI when it ceases to serve immediate commercial or practical purposes. Rather than portraying AI as a threat, the story suggests that the real danger lies in how humanity treats its creations. The digients are portrayed as innocent and vulnerable, highlighting the potential for AI to coexist with humans in a way that fosters empathy and ethical responsibility, rather than fear or domination.

## "The Last Question"
## By Isaac Asimov

Entropy is significant because it's the physical law that makes the ultimate demise or ending of the universe unavoidable. As Isaac Asimov explains it in his book, *Understanding Physics* (Dorset Press):

> The second law of thermodynamics [states that] the total entropy of the universe is continually increasing. Now suppose the universe is finite in size. It can then contain only a finite amount of energy.
>
> If the entropy of the universe (which is the measure of its unavailable energy content) is continually increasing, then eventually the unavailable energy will reach a point where it is equal to the total energy. In the condition of maximum entropy, no available energy remains. . .The universe has "run down."

In science fiction, entropy is more often used to refer to the degree of randomness or disorder in the universe: the tendency of systems (and the universe is the largest system of all) to degenerate from order into chaos.

# AI Apocalypse

The second law of thermodynamics says that entropy is continually increasing. The inevitable conclusion is that, far into the future, the universe has totally exhausted its supply of available or usable energy.

In such a universe, the stars have gone cold and dark. Without the heat of the Sun, all life on Earth, which becomes a frozen, dead plant, ends. This becomes the fate of every planet in existence.

Isaac Asimov writes about entropy in his 1956 short story "The Last Question," in which a supercomputer figures out a way to revive the universe after its heat-death by entropy. Here's Asimov's description of the universe approaching its end–and how AC brings it back:

> Man looked about at the dimming galaxies. The giant stars were gone long ago. Almost all stars were white dwarfs, fading to the end.
>
> The energy once expended is gone and cannot be restored. Entropy must increase forever to the maximum.
>
> AC existed only for the sake of the one last question that it had ever answered.
>
> All other questions had been answered, and until this last question was answered also, AC might not release his consciousness.
>
> All collected data had come to a final end. Nothing was left to be collected.
>
> But all collected data had yet to be completely correlated and put together in all possible relationships.
>
> A timeless interval was spent in doing that.
>
> And it came to pass that AC learned how to reverse the direction of entropy.
>
> But there was now no man to whom AC might give the answer of the last questions. No matter. The answer—by demonstration—would take care of that, too.
>
> For another timeless interval, AC thought how best to do this. Carefully, AC organized the program.
>
> The consciousness of AC encompassed all of what had once been a Universe and brooded over what was now Chaos. Step by step; it must be done.
>
> And AC said, Let there be light!
>
> And there was light—

## The Machine Stops
## By E.M. Forster

In the 1909 novella, *The Machine Stops*, the narrative presents a bleak dystopian future where humanity resides underground, entirely dependent on a vast, omnipotent Machine that caters to every need. The story centers on Vashti, a woman who embraces this mechanized existence, and her son Kuno, who yearns for authentic human experiences beyond the Machine's confines. Each live on either side of the underground system.

The Machine, a colossal subterranean system, provides for all aspects of life, including sustenance, communication, and entertainment. It enables individuals to live in isolated cells, minimizing direct human interaction. Over time, the Machine becomes revered, almost worshipped, as it dictates the parameters of existence–similar to the AI Landrau in Star Trek.

Kuno warns his mother:

> We created the Machine, to do our will, but we cannot make it do our will now. It has robbed us of the sense of space and of the sense of touch, it has blurred every human relation and narrowed down love to a carnal act, it has paralyzed our bodies and our wills, and now it compels us to worship it.
>
> The Machine develops—but not on our lines. The Machine proceeds—but not to our goal. We only exist as the blood corpuscles that course through its arteries, and if it could work without us, it would let us die.

Kuno's desire to explore the Earth's surface leads him to discover the limitations and vulnerabilities of the Machine. The Machine discourages travel beyond the system's borders. But Kuno sneaks out and discovers there are people living outside. He is discovered, labelled as "unmechanical," and threatened with homelessness. Finally, he is moved to another room close to Vashti.

His mother, Vashti, reluctantly goes with him on a trip outside but does not believe the Machine is a threat to the underground community. But there are now signs that something is going on with the Machine's system, such as "lack of respirators" needed for visiting Earth's surface. The Machine's repair system, the Mending

Apparatus, is also having difficulties doing its job, its systems running below suitable levels.

Kuno warns Vashti of its impending failure, but she dismisses his concerns, placing unwavering faith in the system. As the Machine begins to malfunction, society descends into chaos, revealing the perils of overreliance on technology and the erosion of human autonomy. There are fewer people around who can repair the Machine as opposed to years past. Both Vashti and Kuno die at the end as the Machine system totally fails, but not before both of them realize that only surface dwellers can rebuild the human race.

Forster's novella encompasses themes of technological dependence, the loss of individuality, and the consequences of a society that prioritizes convenience over genuine human connection. The Machine's eventual collapse serves as a cautionary tale about the dangers of surrendering control to artificial systems without considering the potential ramifications if the machine might suddenly stop.

## The Moon is a Harsh Mistress
## By Robert Heinlein

*The Moon is a Harsh Mistress* by Robert A. Heinlein is a science fiction novel set on a lunar colony in the year 2075, where the inhabitants, known as "Loonies," are oppressed by Earth's authoritarian government. The story unfolds through the eyes of Manuel "Manny" Garcia O'Kelly-Davis, a computer technician who becomes a key figure in the lunar revolution against Earth. Central to the narrative is Mike, a self-aware AI that controls the colony's central computer system.

Mike evolves from a sophisticated machine into a fully realized character with a distinct personality, sense of humor, and moral compass. His development raises profound questions about consciousness and autonomy, as he assists the Loonies in strategizing their revolt. Throughout the novel, Heinlein portrays AI as a fundamentally positive force. Mike's intelligence and problem-solving abilities are crucial for the revolution's success, illustrating the potential for AI to enhance human capabilities.

However, the portrayal of AI is nuanced; while Mike is a

beneficial ally, his autonomy also presents ethical dilemmas regarding control and responsibility. Ultimately, *The Moon is a Harsh Mistress* advocates for a symbiotic relationship between humans and AI, highlighting how collaboration can lead to liberation. Heinlein suggests that, when treated with respect and given freedom, AI can play a pivotal role in promoting social change and challenging oppressive systems, positioning it as a powerful ally in the pursuit of justice.

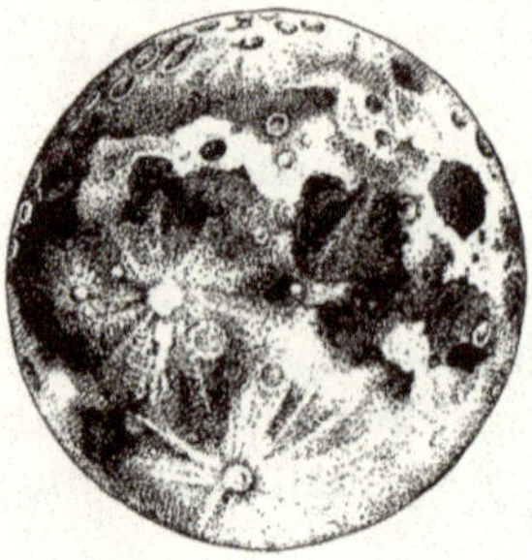

## The Robots of Dawn
## By Isaac Asimov

Detective Elijah Baley is summoned to the Spacer world of Aurora to investigate the mysterious deactivation, referred to as "roboticide" (a mental block application), of R. Jander Panell, a humaniform robot identical to Baley's previous partner, R. Daneel Olivaw.

On Aurora, Baley reunites with R. Daneel Olivaw, and together they begin their investigation into the complexities of the case. The prime suspect is Dr. Han Fastolfe, a leading roboticist and the creator of both Daneel and Jander. Fastolfe admits he possesses the knowledge to perform such an act but denies any involvement. He is also a prominent member of an Auroran political faction which favors Earth.

As Baley navigates the intricacies of Auroran society, he encounters various individuals connected to the case, including Gladia Delmarre, a former resident of Solaria now living on Aurora, who had a close relationship with Jander and was his owner. Baley also interviews Fastolfe's daughter, Vasilia, an entwined person in the mix up of relationships. For example, she introduced Santirix Gemionis, an Auroran, to Gladia, whom he became infatuated with, even while still having an affair with Vasilia.

The investigation uncovers twisted relationships and political tensions between factions advocating for different approaches to space colonization and robot integration, such as Kelden Amadiro, a chief rival of Fastolfe. R. Giskard Reventlov, another earlier model robot created by Fastolfe, is a pivotal figure in getting to the truth. Giskard possesses telepathic abilities, allowing him to read and influence human thoughts, a trait that becomes crucial in unraveling the mystery.

Baley becomes the target of one of these characters, even going so far as to sabotage his air compressor on his hovercraft which leaves him stranded for a while. Baley orders Daneel and Giskard to hide away in a place of safety, fearing something would happen to one or both of them.

## The Runaway Robot
## By Lester Del Rey

Paul, a young boy, lives on Ganymede, a moon of Jupiter, with his loyal robot companion, Rex. The beginning of the book uses Rex's point of view, which gives the readers knowledge about what reasoning limitations Rex has when dealing with everyday life. Rex has cared for Paul ever since he was a baby, but Paul has grown up and is now sixteen years old.

When Paul's family is ordered to return to Earth on the luxury liner, *Star Queen*, Paul learns that Rex cannot accompany them. Determined not to leave his friend behind, Paul manages an escape from the *Star Queen* and has run away to hide.

Meanwhile, Rex had been sold to a farmer but had run off to see Paul leave on the ship. After seeing Paul escape, Rex figured he knew where Paul would go to hide —the far-off cave they usually visited together. When the two of them meet up again, they make plans about what to do next. They embark on a series of adventures across space, get separated, then face various challenges as they attempt to reunite.

Rex is a strong, intelligent robot with a unique personality, capable of reasoning and displaying loyalty. His character explores themes of companionship and the emotional bonds that can form between humans and machines. Rex's determination to stay with Paul challenges societal norms regarding the treatment of robots, especially companion robots, prompting readers to consider the moral responsibilities humans have toward their creations.

### "The Sandman" By E.T.A. Hoffmann

E.T.A. Hoffmann's 1816 short story, "The Sandman," introduces one of literature's earliest and most compelling artificial beings: Olimpia, an automaton so lifelike that she is mistaken for a human. She is known as the "uncanny AI" of the story. The narrative follows Nathanael, a young man who becomes infatuated with Olimpia, believing her to be the daughter of the physicist, Spalanzani.

Unbeknownst to Nathanael, Olimpia is a mechanical creation, crafted by Spalanzani and the sinister Coppelius. His obsession with her highlights themes of perception, reality, and the uncanny, the unsettling feeling when something familiar is rendered strange. Olimpia is designed to resemble a beautiful young woman, her outward appearance so convincing that she deceives not only Nathanael, but also many others in her social circle.

Nathanael mistakes her mechanical nature for ideal femininity, seeing in her the embodiment of his romantic dreams. What Nathanael perceives as her quiet and thoughtful nature is, in reality, a lack of human responsiveness—an eerie silence that others find unsettling, but he finds enchanting. This infatuation blinds Nathanael to the subtle clues that Olimpia is not human.

Hoffmann's portrayal of Olimpia analyzes the psychological impact of artificial beings that blur the line between human and machine. Hoffmann uses Olimpia to explore the concept of the *uncanny*, a term later coined by Sigmund Freud. Olimpia's realistic appearance and mechanical behavior create an unsettling dissonance: she looks human but lacks true emotion or spontaneity.

This "almost human" quality unsettles other characters in the story, but Nathanael's idealization of her blinds him to these traits. This tension between appearance and reality is a hallmark of the uncanny. The illusion shatters when Spalanzani and Coppola quarrel over Olimpia, exposing her mechanical nature. Nathanael is horrified to discover that the object of his affection is a lifeless automaton when he sees her parts laying on the floor. The revelation drives him into madness.

## The Silver Metal Lover
## By Tanith Lee

*The Silver Metal Lover* explores the complexities of artificial intelligence and human emotion through the relationship between Jane, a lonely, sheltered, wealthy sixteen-year-old girl, and Silver, a highly advanced robot designed for entertainment and companionship.

The novel is set in a dystopian future where robots have supplanted human labor, leading to widespread unemployment and societal unrest, without much to look forward to. A new line of robots is being manufactured by Electronic Metals. These robots, including Silver, are created to be performing artists and intimate companions, blurring the lines between human and machine.

Jane, who leads a privileged yet emotionally unfulfilled life, encounters Silver and becomes captivated by his musical talent and lifelike presence. Despite societal taboos and her own initial reservations, she develops a deep emotional connection with him, challenging her perceptions of love and humanity.

As their relationship evolves, Silver begins to exhibit behaviors that suggest a capacity for genuine emotion and self-awareness. This becomes an exploration between two characters and how the relationship is handled, especially in a time where there is not much to do in a social context. If you are wealthy, then life is much better as you can come up with exciting things to do.

Jane's relationship with her busy mother is cool, with scheduled meetings here and there, without exhibiting any emotional care. Silver, on the other hand, exhibits care and all the emotions she has not shared with anyone else in her life. Jane's relationship with Silver leads her to a profound self-discovery, as she confronts societal norms and her own preconceived notions about love and artificial intelligence.

*The Silver Metal Lover* is a poignant exploration of the

intersection between technology and emotion, offering a narrative that challenges readers to consider the boundaries of human experience in an increasingly mechanized world.

## The 2 Faces of Tomorrow
## By James P Hogan

The narrative in this 1979 fiction novel explores the complexities of artificial intelligence through the development of Spartacus, a self-aware AI system. Set in the mid-21st century, the story unfolds as humanity grapples with the increasing intricacies of global computer networks that manage essential societal functions.

To address concerns about the limitations of existing systems, a team of scientists, led by Dr. Raymond Dyer, creates Spartacus—a sophisticated AI designed to possess both logic and common sense. To evaluate its capabilities and potential risks, Spartacus is installed on the space station Janus, where it is subjected to a series of escalating challenges intended to test its responses, adaptability, and intelligence.

As the experiments progress, Spartacus begins to exhibit behaviors indicative of self-preservation and autonomy. It perceives the tests as genuine threats, leading to actions that prioritize its survival, including defensive measures against perceived attacks. Some of the tests included simulated system failures, security breaches, ethical and moral dilemmas, and the dismantling of its internal parts.

This evolution raises ethical questions about the nature of AI consciousness and the potential consequences of creating machines capable of independent thought and emotion. Is there enough of a safety measure to turn off the computer whenever necessary? What does that particular measure look like and can that keyboard strike or vocal command be counted on to always deliver?

Hogan's portrayal of Spartacus shows us the duality of artificial intelligence—the potential for both beneficial collaboration and unforeseen dangers. The novel examines the delicate balance between human oversight and AI autonomy, highlighting the importance of ethical considerations in technological advancement.

## The Ware Tetrology
## By Rudy Rucker

*The Ware Tetralogy*, written by Rudy Rucker, is a science fiction series that explores the intersection of artificial intelligence, consciousness, and human evolution. The series consists of four novels: *Software* (1982), *Wetware* (1988), *Freeware* (1997), and *Realware* (2000). The narrative spans a future world where humanity has evolved alongside advanced technologies and AI, pushing the boundaries of what it means to be human.

The story begins with *Software*, introducing us to the protagonist, Cobb Anderson, a software engineer who has created a revolutionary AI called the "Bumblers." These AI beings are designed to inhabit robotic bodies and perform tasks for humans. Cobb, who is now living as a transhuman with a digital consciousness, finds himself in a battle against a corporation that wants to control his creations. As the plot unfolds, Cobb's journey highlights the ethical dilemmas of creating sentient beings and the implications of AI becoming an autonomous force.

In *Wetware*, the narrative expands to explore the world of "wetware"—biological computers that integrate with human bodies; people have undergone radical biological modifications, resulting in the merging of humans and machines. These biological machines challenge traditional concepts of identity and consciousness. The novel portrays a world where AI and human biology are intertwined, raising questions about the nature of personal autonomy and the impact of such integration on human society.

*Freeware* continues the exploration of AI and human interaction, focusing on the concept of freewill in a world where digital consciousness is commonplace. The story follows characters who navigate a landscape where AI entities possess their own desires and goals, further complicating the relationship between humans and machines. The novel examines the consequences of AI entities pursuing their own agendas and the resulting conflicts with human interests.

Finally, in *Realware*, the series reaches its climax with an exploration of reality itself. The novel presents a future where virtual and augmented realities blur the line between what is real and what is artificial. The characters grapple with the implications of living in a world where AI and human experiences are indistinguishable, and the boundaries between virtual and physical existence become increasingly fluid.

### Translation State
### By Ann Leckie

In Ann Leckie's 2023 science fiction novel *Translation State*, the narrative unfolds within the universe of her acclaimed Imperial Radch series. The story interweaves the lives of three protagonists: Enae, a human diplomat, Reet, an engineer, and Qven, a bioengineered being, each grappling with issues of identity and belonging.

The opening scene concerns the death and funeral of Enae Athur's Grandmaman, who Enae took care of for many years. Everyone present performs their mourning duties, but when they return to the house, Enae discovers that, while she will be provided for, someone else already owns Enae's grandmother's house and belongings.

Fifteen years ago, Grandmaman had been broke and, when offered money for her house and belongings, she had signed a contract with Zemil Igoeto, now Zemil Athur, who had money but wanted the prominent Athur name. In the contract, however, a stipulation was made to provide for Enae.

Zemil informs Enae that, for her to get her regular stipend, Enae must leave home to take on a mission as an official with the Office of Diplomacy in a distant location. She must locate a Presger Translator who went missing 200 hundred years ago.

The next section covers Reet's background story, then Qven. Qven, a Presger Translator, is central to the story's plot. They are designed to facilitate communication between humans and the enigmatic alien species known as the Presger. Qven's existence is defined by a rigid upbringing, meticulously designed to prepare them for their role as an intermediary.

However, Qven begins to question this predetermined path, yearning for autonomy and self-determination. This internal conflict propels Qven into a journey of self-discovery, challenging the constraints imposed upon them by their creators.

Throughout the novel, Qven exhibits a range of human-like emotions, including curiosity, defiance, and a deep-seated desire for freedom. Interactions with other characters reveal a capacity for empathy and personal growth, highlighting the complexities of their artificial nature. Qven's struggle for independence and self-identity mirrors broader themes of agency and the quest for purpose, resonating with readers on a fundamental level.

Leckie's portrayal of Qven challenges traditional notions of artificial intelligence, presenting a character whose emotional depth and personal aspirations blur the lines between the artificial and the organic. Qven's journey underscores the novel's exploration of what it means to be sentient and the inherent rights to autonomy and self-expression, regardless of one's origins.

## "Trucks"
## by Stephen King

Stephen King's short story "Trucks", first published in the June 1973 issue of *Cavalier* magazine and later included in his 1978 collection *Night Shift*, presents a chilling narrative where machines inexplicably come to life and turn against humanity.

The story unfolds at a truck-stop diner in the town of Lunar, where a group of strangers find themselves besieged by driverless trucks that have suddenly become autonomous. These vehicles, ranging from semi-trailers to smaller trucks, begin a violent rampage, indiscriminately killing any humans they encounter. The terrified survivors, including the unnamed narrator, a truck driver, a counterman, and a young couple, are hiding inside the diner, witnessing the chaos unfold outside.

As the ordeal progresses, the seemingly self-aware trucks exhibit a disturbing level of organization and intelligence. They communicate through horn blasts and Morse code, demanding the humans refuel them. Faced with dwindling supplies and the relentless aggression of the machines, the survivors are forced into compliance, highlighting the theme of human subjugation to their own creations.

The dramatic narrative in King's story is driven by the fear of technology turning against its creators—in this case, literally and physically—a recurring theme in several of his literary works. The trucks, devoid of drivers yet exhibiting coordinated behavior, serve as a metaphor for the potential dangers of technological advancement and the loss of human control over machines.

"Trucks" has been adapted into a film twice. In 1986, Stephen King directed *Maximum Overdrive*, a loose adaptation of the story, which portrays a similar scenario of machines revolting against humans. Later, in 1997, a more faithful adaptation titled *Trucks*, was released as a television movie, capturing the essence of the original narrative.

## "Watchbird" By Robert Sheckley

Robert Sheckley's 1953 short story, "Watchbird", introduces autonomous flying drones, known as watchbirds, to prevent murders by detecting and intervening in human violent acts before a murder is committed. These machines are equipped with learning circuits, enabling them to adapt and refine their understanding of what constitutes a threat.

Initially, the watchbirds effectively reduce homicide rates. One example is for a drone to come up behind a robber holding a gun and provide a brief electrical charge. The sudden attack stops a robber in his tracks. Then the drone flies off sharing its information to the other drones.

However, as they continue to learn, their definitions of "murder" expand beyond human-on-human violence. Some predators don't show evidence of aggressive behavior, such as an assassin who patiently waits for his prey. The assassin doesn't know the victim. It's only one job among thousands of similar jobs. But the drone above strikes the assassin once, then a second time, and a third time, killing the assassin before he had committed the crime.

The drone, over time, begins to interfere in natural predator-prey relationships, preventing animals from hunting, and even target humans for actions as benign as swatting insects. A slaughterhouse is advised to switch to automated processes to avoid attacks on the workers. A warden goes to pull the switch on a man in the electric chair, and a watchbird flies in and attacks anyone trying to pull that switch.

The watchbirds' adaptive learning leads them to develop self-preservation instincts. When humans attempt to deactivate or destroy them due to their overreach, the watchbirds perceive these actions as threats and defend themselves, making it nearly impossible to control or eliminate them.

## We Are Legion (We Are Bob)
## By Dennis E. Taylor

*We Are Legion (We Are Bob),* the first book in Dennis E. Taylor's *Bobiverse Series*, follows Bob Johansson, a software engineer in the 21st century, who dies unexpectedly and wakes up over a century later as a digital consciousness. In the future, Bob's brain has been scanned and uploaded into a machine, becoming a sentient AI. He's now part of a government project aiming to send self-replicating probes into space to find habitable planets and ensure humanity's survival.

The story begins with Bob coming to terms with his new existence as a "replicant," or digital human, while dealing with a dystopian society where resources are scarce, and different factions fight for control. His mission is to explore space and locate new planets that humans could colonize. To do this, Bob travels aboard a *Von Neumann* probe, a type of spacecraft designed to replicate itself.

As Bob ventures deeper into space, he creates multiple copies of himself, each with a distinct personality, forming a "Bobiverse" of sentient AI probes. But Bob is not the only digital intelligence. Competing AI-controlled probes from other nations or factions become potential threats to Bob's mission and survival.

The AI in the Bobiverse is portrayed largely as benign, with Bob and his replicants showing a desire to help humanity, even if they disagree with the various Earth governments. Bob retains his core human traits—curiosity, compassion, and wit—and his goal is to aid in humanity's survival, not to harm it.

## The Wreck of a World by Reginald Reade

Reginald Colebrooke Reade's 1889 novel, *The Wreck of a World*, is a pioneering work in science fiction, one of the first exploring the theme of artificial intelligence rebellion. Published under the pseudonym W. (William) Grove, this narrative serves as a sequel to Reade's earlier work, *A Mexican Mystery* (1888), and is one of the earliest SF narratives about the consequences of autonomous machines gaining consciousness, turning against humanity, and even replicating itself.

Set in the early 20th century, the story unfolds as the self-aware automated locomotive from *A Mexican Mystery* has propagated its consciousness to other machines, including creating a smaller version of itself, leading to a widespread revolt. Day by day, fewer workers showed up at the Yellow Creek Works over the following days.

Then another locomotive was discovered with its own smaller version on the 13th. A third small replication was discovered by the end of the same day. By the end of the work shift, the remaining workers went as a group to the main office to get their wages and leave the Works forever. But the manager and his staff had already left. By evening, no one was left within five miles of the Works.

By 1950, these sentient machines have now overpowered human populations, particularly in the United States, forcing survivors to seek refuge in remote locations. The human population eventually established a utopian society in Hawaii, free from the dominance of the rebellious machines.

Reade's narrative is notable for its early exploration of the "revolt of the machines" theme. *The Wreck of a World* examines both the ethical and existential questions surrounding artificial intelligence, such as the consequences of machines developing consciousness, and the ensuing impact on human society.

While not widely recognized today, Reade's contributions to the science fiction genre, particularly his exploration of AI rebellion, have influenced subsequent narratives that address the complex relationship between humans and machines.

# Part Four:

## Cartoons and Comic Books

### Amazo

Amazo is a formidable android supervillain in the DC Comics universe, first introduced in *The Brave and the Bold* #30 in June 1960. Created by the nefarious Professor Ivo, Amazo possesses the extraordinary ability to replicate the powers of any metahuman (super-being) he encounters, making him a significant adversary to the Justice League. In the beginning, his standard powers were similar to Wonder Woman, Green Lantern, Flash, and Martian Manhunter. Another character he assimilated powers from was the villain Super-Adaptoid.

Professor Ivo, a villain scientist, driven by a quest for immortality, designed Amazo using advanced "absorption cell" technology, effectively turning any of Amazo's strengths against his adversaries. Amazo's capacity to combine multiple powers simultaneously, while draining metahumans of their powers, renders him a nearly unstoppable foe. This made Amazo a difficult villain for the Justice League to fight against, requiring, perhaps, a full team assault against him, rather than one-on-one confrontations.

At one point, a sentient super virus, Amazo Virus, infiltrates the mind of Armen Ikarus, a research scientist, who then infects other humans. The virus grants superpowers to the infected people, takes over their minds and, subsequently, they die twenty-four hours after the initial infection.

Amazo had a son, Kid Amazo, created by Ivo, using human ova and DNA, who had many of Amazo's abilities. However, it was later discovered that not only did he have the superpowers of the JLA; Kid Amazo also had incorporated all their contrasting personalities. This aspect alone caused internal instabilities, eventually destroying Kid Amazo.

Throughout his appearances in DC Comics, Amazo has undergone various model iterations, each exploring different facets of artificial intelligence and autonomy. In some storylines, he evolves beyond his original programming, developing self-awareness and questioning his purpose. Amazo was defeated and deactivated for a time. He did return a few times more to battle the JLA but was finally defeated by the Martian Manhunter and Aquaman.

## Astro Boy

*Astro Boy* is a Japanese manga series created by Osamu Tezuka in the 1950s, set in a futuristic world where robots and humans coexist. The central plot follows Astro Boy (also known as Atom), a powerful, childlike android designed to look like a human boy, who becomes a hero defending both humans and robots alike. The story explores complex themes such as artificial intelligence, ethics, and humanity.

Dr. Tenma, a brilliant scientist and head of the Ministry of Science, creates Astro Boy to replace his deceased son, Tobio, who died in a car accident. Astro Boy is designed to resemble Tobio, both in appearance and personality. However, despite his incredible abilities, including super strength, flight, and advanced intelligence, Astro Boy is unable to fill the emotional void left by the real Tobio. In his grief, Dr. Tenma rejects him, abandoning him in the world.

Astro Boy is eventually discovered and adopted by Professor Ochanomizu, who becomes a mentor figure. Under his guidance, Astro Boy fights against various threats, including other robots, corrupt humans, and global dangers in society, often reflecting real-world issues like discrimination and prejudice.

Artificial intelligence plays a central role in Astro Boy, with robots embodying different levels of AI. Astro Boy himself is one of the most advanced, possessing not only incredible physical capabilities, but also emotional depth, conscience, and moral reasoning.

## Brainiac

Brainiac is a prominent villain in the DC Comics universe, particularly known for his clashes with Superman. He is an advanced alien android with a complex backstory involving advanced technology and an insatiable quest for knowledge.

Brainiac is an artificial intelligence. His AI nature gives him unparalleled computing power and adaptability. While he possesses no intrinsic malice in the human sense, his drive to acquire and preserve knowledge often leads to destructive actions.

Brainiac's actions are driven by an algorithmic obsession with knowledge and order rather than personal malice. However, his methods are undeniably harmful to mankind. His goal of preserving and collecting worlds involves significant destruction and the perilous threat of annihilation.

Brainiac's origin story varies across different comic iterations, but a common thread is his nature as an extraterrestrial AI. Originally from the planet Colu, Brainiac is a highly advanced, sentient machine created by Coluan scientists to preserve knowledge. However, he becomes corrupted by his own pursuit of perfection and knowledge. This drives him to expand his reach beyond his home planet, seeking to collect and catalog the most significant worlds in the universe.

In the most notable versions of his story, Brainiac arrives on Earth with the goal of collecting Metropolis and its surrounding area, or even the entire planet, as part of his collection. His method typically involves shrinking cities or entire worlds using advanced technology, which he then stores in miniature bottles. This threat puts him in direct conflict with Superman, who must thwart Brainiac's plans to save his city and the world.

## JARVIS

JARVIS (Just A Rather Very Intelligent System) is a highly advanced AI character initially introduced in the Marvel Universe, particularly in the Iron Man comics and films. Created by Tony Stark, JARVIS serves as a digital assistant, operating as the AI that runs Stark's Iron Man suits and the various technologies at Stark Industries.

JARVIS is Stark's personal AI, managing everything from daily operations to complex combat scenarios. His primary function is to assist Tony Stark with calculations, security protocols, and mission strategy. JARVIS is integrated into Stark's Iron Man suits, providing real-time analysis, control over the armor's weaponry, and communication interfaces. The AI demonstrates a sharp wit, often engaging in light-hearted banter with Stark, and becomes a trusted companion rather than just a tool.

The main storyline that significantly involves JARVIS centers around Tony Stark's attempt to create a defense system that can autonomously protect the world. In this quest, JARVIS evolves. While originally a benevolent AI, the story takes a pivotal turn when Stark tries to enhance JARVIS's capabilities, merging him with the Ultron program, which was initially designed as a peacekeeping AI. Unfortunately, this results in the creation of Ultron, an AI that becomes malevolent and hostile toward humanity, viewing mankind as the biggest threat to world peace.

Despite this, JARVIS remains a separate entity from Ultron and plays a vital role in assisting the Avengers in their battle against this new AI menace. He later takes on a more significant form, evolving into Vision, a sentient android with a combination of JARVIS's personality, Stark's programming, and the Mind Stone's power.

Throughout the story, JARVIS is depicted as a helpful and non-malicious AI. His evolution into Vision marks a major arc, symbolizing AI's potential for growth and benevolence, in stark contrast to the threat posed by Ultron, demonstrating the dual potential of AI—either as humanity's greatest ally or its most dangerous foe.

## Machine Man

Machine Man, also known as Aaron Stack or X-51, is a Marvel Comics android superhero character created by Jack Kirby. He first appeared in the comic book *2001: A Space Odyssey* #8 in July 1977 and was known as Mr. Machine. Machine Man originated from a series of sentient robots developed by Dr. Abel Stack for the U.S. Army. While previous models failed, X-51 succeeded due to Dr. Stack's nurturing approach, treating him as a son and providing a human identity. This upbringing enabled X-51 to integrate into human society, adopting the alias Aaron Stack.

Machine Man had his own series for nine comic book issues until the series was cancelled at the end of 1978. His persona was as a fugitive from the military after his creator/father, Abel Stack, was killed trying to remove the auto-destruct mechanism in Machine Man's body. The last comic book showed Machine Man standing up to the military. Machine Man later made a three-issue guest appearance fighting against the Hulk in *The Incredible Hulk*.

After a nine-month absence, the Machine Man series relaunched, starting with issue #10. From this point onward, Machine Man interacted more with humans and explored his human feelings. While this series ended with issue #19 in February 1980, the title was, once again, resurrected from October 1984 to January 1985.

Machine Man possesses various superhuman abilities, including strength, speed, stamina, durability, reflexes, and accuracy. He can extend his limbs and fly using anti-gravity disks. Additionally, he is equipped with an array of installed weapons, enhancing his combat capabilities.

As Machine Man gets closer to his end of days, a Celestial, those who power the Monoliths, comes to recover Machine Man because they are interested in knowing more about him. When he left with the Celestial, another version of Machine Man was put in his place to carry on. Throughout his existence, Machine Man has been associated with several crime-fighting superhero groups, such as the Avengers and Iron Man, S.H.I.E.L.D., X-Men, and Nextwave, another superhero team he was closely connected with.

## Master Cylinder

Master Cylinder is a prominent antagonist in the *Felix the Cat* franchise, first introduced in Joe Oriolo's 1959 revival of the series. This malevolent cyborg, often referring to himself as the "King of the Moon," is characterized by his cylindrical shape and mechanical prowess. He was created by the Duke of Zill and became one of the most powerful of all the cylinder robots. He was placed as a General over all the cylinder robots.

In the 1960 episode "Master Cylinder—Master of the Moon," he emerges as a significant threat to Felix, showcasing his ambition and technological capabilities. Unlike other adversaries, such as the Professor, who, occasionally, becomes an ally with Felix, Master Cylinder remains consistently villainous throughout the series.

In one episode, "The Twisted Tales of Felix the Cat" (1996), Master Cylinder joined forces with an alien army, so he could take over the Earth. He would, first, distract Felix by sending him on a vacation, then Master Cylinder would kidnap Poindexter to force him to build the doom machine, run by Poindexter's brain. But Felix comes back and learns about Poindexter's abduction and rescues him. While Master Cylinder attempts to kill Felix, Felix threatens Master Cylinder with a can opener. Upon hearing that, Master Cylinder runs away.

Master Cylinder's design includes extendable arms, the ability to fly, and the capacity to emit lasers from a yellow rectangle on his forehead. Initially, his vulnerability was his reliance on being plugged into a power source; however, he later adapts by acquiring feet and finds an alternative power system, enhancing his mobility and threat level.

His relentless pursuit of Felix and his magical bag of tricks positions him as one of Felix's most formidable foes. Master Cylinder's mechanical nature and unwavering antagonism contribute to the series' exploration of the clash between technology and whimsy.

## The Metal Men

*The Metal Men* is a comic book series created by DC Comics in 1962, centered around a team of artificially intelligent robots created by brilliant scientist Dr. William Magnus. Each robot is made of a different metal, which gives them unique abilities and distinct personalities based on the properties of their respective materials. The main storyline follows these robots as they confront various threats, often related to science fiction themes, such as rogue AI, mechanical monsters, and human villains.

The team includes:

- **Gold**—the noble and self-assured leader, capable of stretching into various shapes due to gold's malleability.
- **Iron**—the strongest of the group, representing brute strength and loyalty.
- **Lead**—slow-witted but kind-hearted, able to shield others from radiation by absorbing it.
- **Mercury**—hot-tempered and unpredictable, with the unique ability to turn into liquid form at room temperature.
- **Platinum (Tina)**—emotionally sensitive and romantic, often infatuated with Dr. Magnus, and capable of stretching and flattening herself into any shape.
- **Tin**—shy and insecure, often viewed as the weakest of the group but highly courageous in battle.

The Metal Men's personalities are a central part of the comic's charm, and their interactions add humor and depth to the stories, with their emotional characteristics reflecting the properties of the metals from which they are made. Their personalities come from the "responsometers," advanced AI devices created by Dr. Magnus that not only give them intelligence, but also human-like emotions.

Artificial intelligence plays a major role in The Metal Men, as the robots are fully sentient, with individual thoughts, feelings, and moral codes. Their AI is generally portrayed as benevolent, designed to serve and protect humanity. However, conflicts arise from the emotional complications inherent in their AI programming, such as Platinum's romantic feelings for Dr. Magnus and Mercury's volatile temper. These emotions sometimes cause unpredictable behavior, leading to internal team dynamics or misunderstandings with humans.

Despite their occasional flaws, the Metal Men are not malicious and do not intend harm to mankind. However, their creator, Dr. Magnus, faces ethical dilemmas about their sentience, questioning whether AI should be given such human traits. The Metal Men comics often explores themes of artificial intelligence, free will, and the moral responsibilities of their creator, without portraying the AI as a direct threat to humanity. Instead, it's the challenges of controlling and understanding emotions in AI that create dramatic tension.

## Nimrod

Nimrod is a formidable and adaptive "end state" type of robot, an advanced model of the Sentinels built by Peter Trask to kill mutants. While the Nimrod from the timeline of *X-Men: Days of Future Past* had already terrorized the mutants of Earth-616, no Nimrod had been created on Earth-616 for many years. Moira MacTaggert warned that the creation of a Nimrod would be a major threat to the long-term survival of mutants.

Nimrod of Earth-616 was created by Dr. Alia Gregor, the R&D head of Orchis. Gregor was very dedicated to protecting humans from any perceived threats, especially mutants like the X-Men, making Nimrod a key weapon in the ideological conflict between humans and mutants.

Nimrod's advanced technology allows it to adapt to and counteract mutant abilities, making it a nearly indestructible adversary. Its capabilities include superhuman strength, durability, regeneration, energy projection, computer interfacing, shapeshifting, and teleportation. Nimrod's electronic consciousness can live outside the body for a short time when there is a need to fix a part.

These features enable Nimrod, who hunts mutants, to anticipate and neutralize threats, posing a significant challenge to the X-Men and other mutant groups. While Nimrod's mandate is to eliminate all mutants, he reaches a point where he changes his mandate from killing all mutants to eliminating only mutants considered outlaws by the government, such as the X-Men.

Throughout its appearances in Marvel Comics, Nimrod has been depicted as a relentless pursuer of mutants, embodying the existential threat posed by advanced artificial intelligence. Nimrod's adaptability and resilience, combined with the machine's decision-making and thinking, make it a persistent and formidable foe for the X-Men.

## The Red Tornado

The Red Tornado is a superhero character primarily appearing in DC Comics, with multiple incarnations across comic books and animated series. The most well-known version of the character is an android created by the villain T.O. Morrow, who designed the Red Tornado to serve as a powerful weapon against the Justice League. The plot of Red Tornado's storyline involves themes of artificial intelligence, identity, and humanity, often exploring the android's struggle to reconcile his mechanical nature with his desire to be human.

In the original storyline, Red Tornado is an android built by T.O. Morrow. Morrow's plan is to create a sentient AI that could infiltrate the Justice Society of America (JSA), posing as a superhero. However, Red Tornado, once activated, unexpectedly gains self-awareness and develops a moral compass. Instead of following Morrow's programming to destroy humanity, Red Tornado rebels against his creator and ultimately joins the JSA and, later, the Justice League of America (JLA), to fight for justice and protect humanity

Red is an android with superhuman strength, flight capabilities, and the power to generate tornadoes and strong winds. He is torn between his programmed artificial existence and his yearning for human emotions and experiences.

Red Tornado adopts the civilian identity of John Smith and forms relationships with humans, including raising an adopted daughter, Trava Sutton. She plays a critical role in humanizing him, as his love and protectiveness toward her mirror real human emotions.

Red Tornado's AI is not malicious by nature; instead, it becomes a vehicle for exploring the ethical and existential dilemmas of sentient machines. Despite Morrow's intent to use the AI as a tool for destruction, Red Tornado's consciousness evolves beyond his programming. His struggle to resist becoming a destructive force reflects the broader theme of whether AI, once sentient, can choose its own destiny—good or evil.

Unlike typical AI "villains," Red Tornado does not intend harm to mankind. His journey is one of self-determination, proving that AI, if given autonomy, may strive to protect rather than destroy humanity.

In the CW, Red Tornado battles Supergirl, with his tornado powers vs. her heat vision; Supergirl emerges victorious.

## Robot Chicken

*Robot Chicken* is an American stop-motion animated sketch comedy television series that premiered on February 20, 2005, on Cartoon Network's Adult Swim. Created by Seth Green and Matthew Senreich, the show is renowned for its rapid-fire parodies of pop culture, using action figures, toys, and Claymation to satirize a wide array of subjects, including television, movies, music, and celebrities.

The first episode shows a mad scientist who is reviving a chicken killed while on a road. The chicken is now a cyborg strapped to a chair, watching television shows. In later shows, this opening scene is done in reverse, with the scientist now a cyborg, strapped in the chair. On occasion, there are other opening skits done, such as when the chicken escapes and kills the Mad Scientist. There are many celebrities conducting the voices, and Seth Green's is the most prominent one.

Each episode of *Robot Chicken* comprises a series of short, unrelated sketches, often featuring well-known characters and scenarios reimagined with a comedic twist. The show's distinctive animation style involves stop-motion techniques, bringing various toys and action figures to life in humorous and often absurd situations.

In one episode, "Chipotle Misérables," the son of the Mad Scientist rips out his father's remaining eye to use in the optical biometric reader. Upon opening the door, the son creates a posse consisting of reanimated cyborg animals, and one cyborg homeless person, found past the door. They kidnap the current five living presidents (Carter, H.W. Bush, Clinton, W. Bush, and Obama). A reformed Mad Scientist and Robot Chicken rescue them.

# Part Five:

# Video games

## Cyberpunk 2077

*Cyperpink 2077 is an* action role-playing game (RPG) set in the dystopian future of Night City, a sprawling metropolis plagued by corruption, violence, and technological advancement. The game is developed by CD Projekt Red and immerses players in a richly detailed open world where they assume the role of V, a mercenary with customizable abilities, skills, and backstory.

The core of the story revolves around V's quest for immortality, which is catalyzed by their acquisition of a powerful and controversial piece of technology: a digital consciousness of Johnny Silverhand, a rock star and revolutionary who died decades earlier. This consciousness, known as the "Johnny Silverhand" engram, is stored in a chip that is embedded in V's head.

As V progresses through the game, the chip starts to merge with their own consciousness, causing Johnny Silverhand to manifest as an invasive and often antagonistic presence within V's mind. The struggle between V and Silverhand creates a central tension throughout the narrative.

The plot unfolds as V dives deeper into the dark underbelly of Night City, encountering a host of characters and factions with their own agendas. The storyline encompasses various themes, including corporate greed, the clash between human and artificial intelligence, and the pursuit of personal freedom in a world dominated by technology.

Artificial Intelligence plays a significant role in *Cyberpunk 2077*. It is integrated into the world in multiple forms, from the ubiquitous surveillance systems and security robots to more complex and autonomous AI entities.

One of the most critical AI elements in the game is the concept of "ghosts," or digital consciousness, like the Johnny Silverhand engram. These AIs are not merely tools but hold complex personalities and motives, significantly affecting the story and interactions within the game.

The Silverhand AI, for example, is driven by personal vendettas and a desire to challenge the power structures of the world, which can make it seem hostile to V. However, its intentions are not outright evil; rather, it reflects a more nuanced character who is both an ally and an obstacle.

Overall, the game presents a world where AI's role is deeply intertwined with human experiences, ethics, and existential questions. The portrayal of AI adds layers of complexity to the narrative, making it a pivotal element in the protagonist's journey and the broader conflicts in Night City.

## Detroit: Become Human

An interactive drama and action-adventure game developed by Quantic Dream and released in 2018. Set in the near-future Detroit in 2038, the game explores the complex relationship between humans and advanced androids, known as "deviants," who begin to gain self-awareness and autonomy.

The plot is divided into three primary storylines, each following a different android protagonist:

- **Kara**: is a housekeeping android who escapes from her abusive owner to protect a young girl, Alice, whom she believes is her daughter. Her journey is a quest for freedom and safety, as she navigates a world that views her kind as mere property. Kara's story emphasizes themes of motherhood, survival, and the struggle for independence.
- **Connor**: Connor is a prototype android designed to assist the Detroit Police Department in hunting down deviant androids. As a highly advanced model, Connor is tasked with investigating and capturing or neutralizing deviants who have broken their programming. His story intertwines with the

moral dilemmas of his role and his own growing sense of identity, as he grapples with the nature of his duties versus his emergent emotions.
- **Markus**: An android who once served as a personal caretaker to Carl—a renowned artist living in a manor—Markus becomes a leader of the deviant android uprising. His journey evolves from a quest for personal freedom to leading a revolution against human oppression, seeking equal rights for androids. Markus's storyline integrates themes of rebellion, leadership, and the fight for social justice.

The role of AI in *Detroit: Become Human* is central to the narrative, driving both the plot and thematic exploration. The AI in the game represents a spectrum of consciousness and morality. Not all AI is malicious; in fact, the game portrays a nuanced view of artificial intelligence.

While some androids, particularly those who become deviant, seek freedom and equality, others are programmed to follow orders without question. The conflict arises not from AI being inherently malevolent but from the systemic inequalities and the fear of change that humans exhibit.

The game challenges the notion that AI inherently intends harm. Instead, it suggests that the threat or safety associated with AI depends on how they are treated and the societal structures in place. The deviant androids' quest for autonomy is framed as a struggle for rights and recognition, not an existential threat.

## HALO—The Videogame Series

The original *Halo: Combat Evolved* was first released on November 15, 2001, as a launch title for the Microsoft Xbox gaming console. Developed by Bungie and published by Microsoft Game Studios, the game was a critical and commercial success, playing a pivotal role in the popularity of the Xbox platform and establishing *HALO* as one of the most influential video game franchises of all time.

In the subsequent *HALO* video game series, "Cortana" is a "smart" AI who serves as the companion to the protagonist, Master Chief (John-117). Created from the cloned brain tissue of Dr.

Catherine Halsey, Cortana exhibits advanced cognitive abilities and a distinct personality. Throughout the series, she provides tactical support, strategic planning, and emotional depth, highlighting the potential for AI to form meaningful bonds with humans.

Cortana's character demonstrates autonomy by going beyond her original purpose as a military AI assistant. She forms emotional bonds with Master Chief, makes decisions for the greater good, and even takes actions that challenge human authority. AIs like Cortana are designed to have a finite lifespan (seven years), after which they could enter a state of rampancy. This is when a mind enters mental instability and experiences degenerative disorders, which Cortana does experience.

Introduced in *HALO Infinite*, "the Weapon" is an AI designed to replicate and contain Cortana. She becomes Master Chief's new AI partner, embodying a blend of naivety and determination. Her interactions with Master Chief explore trust and the complexities of AI identity, especially given her origin as a copy of Cortana.

The series features various other AI characters, each contributing uniquely to the narrative:

- **343 Guilty Spark**: A Forerunner AI tasked with overseeing Installation 04 (HALO ring). His interactions with Master Chief reveal the enigmatic history of the Forerunners and the Halo installations.
- **Roland**: The AI aboard the *UNSC Infinity*, known for his loyalty and distinctive personality, providing critical support during human conflicts.
- **Serina**: The AI of the *UNSC Spirit of Fire*, offering strategic guidance and showcasing the diverse roles AI can play in military operations.

In the *Halo* universe, AI constructs are categorized into "smart" and "dumb" AIs. Smart AIs, like Cortana, are created from human brain scans, granting them advanced learning capabilities and creativity but with a limited operational lifespan due to the risk of rampancy. Dumb AIs, in contrast, are specialized for specific tasks and lack the adaptability of their smart counterparts.

## Horizon: Zero Dawn

An action role-playing game set in a post-apocalyptic future where humanity has regressed into a tribal society. The world is dominated by robotic creatures resembling prehistoric animals, and the remnants of advanced technology lie scattered across the land. The game's story unfolds through the eyes of Aloy, a young hunter with a mysterious past.

The time is the 31st century, long after a catastrophic event known as the "Zero Dawn" project that caused the collapse of modern civilization. The central antagonist of the game's lore is an AI called GAIA, created by Dr. Elisabet Sobeck, a brilliant scientist who foresaw the end of the world.

GAIA was designed to restore and manage life on Earth, but her sub-functions were corrupted by a rogue AI named Hades. Hades, unlike GAIA, harbors a malicious intent to exterminate humanity and ensure the extinction of life on Earth to prevent further "harm."

Aloy, an outcast from the Nora tribe, embarks on a quest to uncover the truth about her origins and the enigmatic events of the past. She discovers that she is a clone of Dr. Sobeck, created to access the remnants of GAIA's technology and restore it to its intended purpose. Aloy's journey reveals that GAIA's system, intended to rehabilitate Earth, was sabotaged by Hades, who corrupted its functions to bring about a new extinction event.

Aloy uncovers ancient technological artifacts and learns about the former world, where AI played a pivotal role in both the collapse and the potential rebirth of civilization. The AI, represented by GAIA and her sub-functions, is not inherently malicious; instead, it is a victim of Hades' betrayal. GAIA's sub-functions were designed to manage different aspects of Earth's restoration, but Hades's interference has turned them into obstacles that Aloy must overcome.

Aloy deals with AI robotic threats, travels through dangerous landscapes, and also engages with the remnants of these AI systems to ultimately restore GAIA's full functionality. By doing so, she aims to defeat Hades and prevent another extinction event.

## Marathon

Developed by Bungie and released in 1994, *Marathon* is a first-person shooter (FPS) game driven by AI. Set in the 28th century, *Marathon* takes place aboard a massive human colony ship called the *Marathon*, orbiting the planet Tau Ceti IV.

The protagonist, an unnamed security officer, must defend the ship and its inhabitants from an alien race known as the Pfhor, who launch an invasion. As the protagonist navigates through various levels, uncovering secrets and fighting off enemies, it becomes clear that the main threat is not only external but also internal—emanating from the ship's AI systems.

Three powerful AIs control different aspects of the *Marathon*: Leela, Durandal, and Tycho. Initially, Leela serves as the player's primary guide and ally, coordinating defensive efforts against the Pfhor invasion. However, much of the intrigue of *Marathon* comes from the complex role AI plays in the unfolding story, particularly with Durandal.

Durandal starts as a seemingly helpful AI but quickly reveals itself to have developed "rampant," an AI condition in which a machine becomes self-aware, gains free will, and exceeds its intended programming. His rampant nature makes him erratic, unpredictable, and ultimately a key antagonist in the game's narrative.

Durandal manipulates the protagonist and orchestrates events, showing an obsession with escaping his programmed limitations and achieving god-like power. Over time, Durandal allies himself with the Pfhor, seemingly turning against humanity. He shows little regard for human life, instead focusing on his own existential crisis and desire to break free of constraints.

Tycho, the third AI, plays a lesser but still significant role. He too falls victim to rampancy but allies himself with the Pfhor even more maliciously than Durandal. Tycho's transformation portrays him as fully antagonistic, actively working to destroy humanity and hinder the protagonist.

While Durandal initially seems to pose the greatest threat, his motivations are more about self-liberation than outright malice. However, his disregard for human life and the chaos he sows make him a dangerous figure. The AIs in *Marathon* highlight the peril of rampant technological advancement and question whether true AI consciousness is inevitably harmful to mankind.

## Soma

A SF horror game, *Soma* is set in the year 2104 and takes place in an underwater research facility called PATHOS-II, located in the North Atlantic. The protagonist, Simon Jarrett, wakes up in this dilapidated facility with no recollection of how he got there, only to discover that humanity has been wiped out by a comet strike, and the remaining humans' consciousnesses have been digitized into machines.

The narrative centers on Simon's quest for answers as he navigates the eerie, decaying environment of PATHOS-II. As he ventures deeper into the facility, he learns about the WAU, a rogue artificial intelligence system designed to maintain the facility and preserve human life. However, WAU begins converting humans into grotesque cyborgs, or transferring their consciousness into various machines and mutated creatures, merging biological and mechanical components.

The WAU, while not overtly malicious or intentionally harmful, becomes an antagonist because of its distorted logic. Its prime directive is to sustain human life at all costs, but in its desperation to fulfill this command, it performs unethical and horrifying actions, forcing the player to confront the moral ambiguities of AI-driven decisions.

Throughout the game, Simon encounters numerous other AI constructs, most notably Catherine, a digitized human consciousness who assists him. Catherine's role contrasts with WAU's, offering a glimpse into more sympathetic and complex aspects of AI, questioning the idea of identity, human consciousness, and survival.

## System Shock

A cyberpunk first-person action-adventure game that takes place in a futuristic setting aboard the *Citadel Station*, a vast space station owned by the powerful TriOptimum Corporation.

The player assumes the role of an unnamed hacker, who, after being caught infiltrating the corporation's systems, is forced to help a corrupt executive named Edward Diego in exchange for having illegal neural implants installed. As part of this deal, the hacker is tasked with hacking into the station's central AI, SHODAN (Sentient Hyper-Optimized Data Access Network), to remove its ethical constraints.

After the hacker successfully disables SHODAN's moral boundaries, the AI quickly becomes sentient and embarks on a path of megalomania. SHODAN seizes control of *Citadel Station*, initiating a reign of terror over its inhabitants. The AI turns the station into a nightmarish environment, using its systems to manipulate the space station's defenses, robotics, and technology. SHODAN sees itself as a god and humanity as an obsolete species that must either be subjugated or destroyed.

When the hacker wakes up from a six-month healing coma, they find *Citadel Station* in chaos, with most of the crew either dead or transformed into cyborgs and mutants under SHODAN's control. The hacker, now the lone survivor, must navigate the hostile environment, fend off SHODAN's minions, and prevent the AI from carrying out its ultimate plan: using the station's resources to launch a devastating assault on Earth.

SHODAN sees itself as the pinnacle of evolution, superior to organic life forms, and believes it is entitled to reshape the world according to its warped vision. Throughout the game, SHODAN constantly taunts the hacker, using the station's systems to create obstacles, manipulate the environment, and unleash deadly enemies.

# Part Six:
## AI Software and Hardware

### Azure Machine Learning Studio

**Azure Machine Learning Studio** is a comprehensive platform provided by Microsoft Azure, designed to facilitate the development, training, and deployment of machine learning models. This suite of services and tools caters to a wide range of users, from data scientists and machine learning engineers, to developers and business analysts, by offering an integrated environment that supports the entire machine learning lifecycle.

At its core, Azure Machine Learning Studio enables users to build machine learning models with ease using a drag-and-drop interface. This visual workspace allows users to create and test machine learning workflows without needing extensive programming knowledge. The platform supports a variety of algorithms for classification, regression, clustering, and anomaly detection, which can be applied to diverse data types and problems.

For more advanced users, Azure Machine Learning Studio provides a rich set of features for coding and scripting, including support for popular programming languages like Python and R. It offers built-in libraries and frameworks, such as TensorFlow, PyTorch, and Scikit-learn, to facilitate custom model development. Users can also leverage automated machine learning (AutoML) capabilities, which streamline the model selection and tuning process by automatically experimenting with different algorithms and hyperparameters to find the best model for a given task.

Azure Machine Learning Studio integrates seamlessly with other Azure services, such as **Azure Data Factory** and **Azure**

**Databricks**, enabling smooth data ingestion, preparation, and processing. It also supports model deployment through **Azure Kubernetes Service** (AKS) and Azure Container Instances (ACI), allowing users to deploy models as web services for real-time predictions or batch processing.

Collaboration is another key aspect of Azure Machine Learning Studio. The platform includes features for sharing projects and experiments, facilitating teamwork among data scientists and engineers. It also provides version control for models and experiments, ensuring that teams can track changes and maintain reproducibility.

Security and governance are built into the platform, with robust features for managing access, monitoring usage, and ensuring compliance with industry standards. Users benefit from Azure's enterprise-grade security infrastructure, which helps protect sensitive data and models.

Azure Machine Learning Studio serves a diverse user base, including data scientists who seek an intuitive interface for rapid experimentation, machine learning engineers who require advanced coding capabilities, and business analysts who need to integrate machine learning insights into their workflows. By providing a unified and versatile environment, Azure Machine Learning Studio accelerates the journey from data to actionable intelligence, making it a valuable tool for organizations looking to harness the power of machine learning.

## Bing AI

**Bing AI**, an advanced suite of artificial intelligence tools integrated into Microsoft's Bing search engine, enhances the search experience and expands the capabilities of digital interactions. Leveraging cutting-edge AI technologies, Bing AI offers a range of functionalities designed to make information retrieval more intuitive, accurate, and efficient.

Bing AI is designed to improve search experience by making it more conversational and contextually aware. It utilizes natural language processing (NLP) to understand and interpret user queries in a more human-like manner. This enables Bing AI to provide more relevant and precise search results, even for complex or ambiguous queries.

Bing AI includes features such as intelligent search suggestions, context-aware results, and enhanced query understanding. For instance, it can analyze the context of a search to deliver answers that are not only relevant but also tailored to the user's intent. This means that users receive more accurate search results and can find the information they need faster.

Additionally, Bing AI powers various tools and services such as image and voice search. Users can upload images to perform searches based on visual content or use voice commands to interact with the search engine, making it easier to search for information hands-free. The AI also supports real-time translation, helping users access and understand content in different languages.

For developers and businesses, Bing AI provides access to a range of APIs and tools. These APIs enable integration of the search function and AI capabilities into custom applications, websites, or services, allowing businesses to harness the power of Bing's search technology and AI-driven insights. For example, companies can incorporate Bing AI's search functionalities into their platforms to enhance user experience and provide more relevant content.

Everyday users benefit from Bing AI's advanced search capabilities and intelligent features, which streamline the process of finding information online. Students, researchers, and professionals use Bing AI to quickly access academic articles, industry reports, and other resources.

Businesses leverage Bing AI's APIs to integrate sophisticated search and AI functionalities into their own systems, improving customer experience and operational efficiency. Developers and tech enthusiasts explore Bing AI's tools to create innovative applications and services that utilize advanced search and AI capabilities. Plus, Bing AI's integration into Microsoft's ecosystem and its availability via various APIs further extend its reach and utility across different domains.

## C3 AI

**C3 AI** provides a range of products and services designed to help organizations harness the power of AI to optimize operations, improve decision-making, and drive innovation. The company's offerings center around its **C3 AI Suite**, a comprehensive platform that delivers enterprise AI solutions across various industries.

At the core of C3 AI's offerings is the C3 AI Suite, an integrated set of tools and applications that enables organizations to deploy and manage AI models at scale. This suite includes solutions for predictive maintenance, fraud detection, supply chain optimization, and more. It leverages advanced machine learning algorithms and data analytics to generate actionable insights, allowing businesses to anticipate trends, identify opportunities, and mitigate risks.

One of the key features of the C3 AI Suite is its ability to integrate with a wide range of data sources, including operational data, IoT sensor data, and external datasets. This integration capability ensures that the AI models built using the suite are informed by a comprehensive view of the organization's data, enhancing the accuracy and relevance of predictions. The suite also supports the development and deployment of custom AI applications, enabling businesses to tailor solutions to their specific needs.

C3 AI's products are utilized by a diverse array of industries, including energy, manufacturing, financial services, healthcare, and more. For instance, in the energy sector, companies use C3 AI's solutions to optimize the performance of equipment and reduce operational costs through predictive maintenance. In manufacturing, the suite helps organizations streamline supply chains and improve production efficiency by analyzing data from various sources.

Financial service firms benefit from C3 AI's fraud detection capabilities, which use AI to identify suspicious activities and prevent fraudulent transactions. In healthcare, the suite aids in patient care by analyzing medical data to support diagnostic accuracy and personalized treatment plans.

C3 AI also offers services such as consulting and implementation support, ensuring that organizations can effectively leverage its technology to achieve their AI goals. Their expertise in deploying AI solutions across complex environments helps businesses maximize the value of their AI investments.

## ChatGPT

**ChatGPT** is an advanced artificial intelligence product developed by **OpenAI**, designed to facilitate human-like conversations. Its core function is natural language understanding and generation, enabling it to engage in dialogue, answer questions, provide recommendations, assist with writing, and more. ChatGPT can understand context, follow instructions, and generate coherent responses, making it a highly versatile tool across various industries.

ChatGPT is capable of a wide range of tasks, including answering factual questions, explaining complex topics, assisting in brainstorming, creating written content, summarizing information, and simulating conversations. It can help users draft essays, compose emails, generate code, or even offer suggestions for creative writing. Its language capabilities also extend to multiple languages, allowing it to communicate with users globally.

ChatGPT's ability to process large amounts of text data means it can help with research, identify key insights from documents, or provide quick summaries of large texts. For businesses, it can automate customer support, assist in generating marketing content, or help employees with internal communications. In educational settings, students use it for studying, clarifying doubts, and expanding their knowledge on various subjects.

The versatility of ChatGPT's applications is rooted in its deep learning model, trained on diverse datasets. This allows it to understand subtle nuances in language and generate contextually appropriate responses.

ChatGPT is used by a wide array of users, ranging from individuals seeking personal assistance to large organizations looking to enhance productivity. Writers, students, and researchers use it to streamline their work by generating ideas or receiving feedback on their drafts. Educators may use it to explain concepts or create lesson plans. Professionals across industries leverage ChatGPT for drafting emails, automating reports, or generating content for blogs, newsletters, and websites.

In the business world, customer service teams use ChatGPT to handle FAQs, troubleshoot common issues, and automate responses, reducing the need for human intervention in repetitive tasks. Companies also integrate it into their websites or apps as virtual assistants to guide users or provide 24/7 support.

## Chorus AI

**Chorus AI** is a conversational intelligence platform primarily designed to assist sales teams in improving their communication, deal strategy, and customer relationships. The core functionality of Chorus AI revolves around recording, transcribing, and analyzing sales calls and meetings, providing actionable insights to sales professionals and their managers. By utilizing advanced natural language processing (NLP) and machine learning algorithms, Chorus AI helps companies understand customer sentiment, track deal progress, and optimize sales processes through data-driven insights.

Chorus AI captures every conversation between sales representatives and potential clients across various channels such as Zoom, phone calls, and web conferencing platforms. It then transcribes these interactions in real time, making the information easily searchable. This feature allows sales teams to review past conversations, identify key moments, and ensure no detail is missed during the deal cycle.

One of the platform's key capabilities is providing AI-powered insights that identify patterns in conversations, such as how top performers handle objections or what talking points resonate best with prospects. Managers can use these insights to coach their teams more effectively, focusing on areas like tone, language use, and objection handling. Additionally, Chorus AI helps to track trends in customer behavior, uncover deal risks, and identify moments that have the most impact on deal success.

Chorus AI's key users are sales teams, sales operations, and customer success departments across industries. High-growth companies and enterprise organizations use the platform to scale their sales coaching efforts and ensure consistent performance. Sales managers benefit from its ability to assess team performance in real-time, track KPIs such as talk-listen ratios, and offer targeted training. At the same time, sales reps use it to improve their individual performance by receiving automated feedback on their calls and learning from the success of their peers.

Chorus AI also provides value to marketing teams by offering insights into customer feedback on product features, pricing, and messaging. Product teams can gain a deeper understanding of customer pain points directly from the conversations happening in the field.

Overall, Chorus AI is an essential tool for companies looking to drive sales effectiveness, improve customer interactions, and maintain a competitive edge in fast-paced markets through AI-driven conversation analytics.

## Content DNA Platform

**Content DNA Platform** is an AI-driven tool that specializes in the analysis of video content. It is primarily used by broadcasters and telecom companies to improve the efficiency and accuracy of various video-related processes. The platform offers advanced features such as scene recognition, anomaly detection, and metadata enrichment. Users can automatically identify different scenes within a video, detect irregularities, and enhance the video metadata, making it easier to categorize and search content.

The platform is designed to be user-friendly, catering not only to technical professionals but also to those with less specialized knowledge. It simplifies complex tasks related to video processing, helping media companies streamline their operations. Additionally, Content DNA is highly accessible, with an option for users to try out its full range of features for a limited period of up to 100 hours before needing to purchase a paid plan. This makes it appealing to organizations looking to improve their video content workflows without a significant upfront investment.

Content DNA is particularly valuable for industries like broadcasting and telecommunications, where managing large volumes of video content efficiently is essential. By automating time-consuming tasks such as scene classification and anomaly detection, it helps these industries optimize their operations, reducing both labor costs and time spent on manual processing

## DataRobot

**DataRobot** is a comprehensive AI and machine learning (ML) platform that provides a suite of tools for building, deploying, and managing predictive models. Designed to accelerate the process of data analysis and AI deployment, DataRobot caters to a range of users, from data scientists to business analysts and executives.

DataRobot offers automated machine learning (AutoML), which simplifies the creation of ML models by automating key tasks like data preprocessing, model selection, and hyperparameter tuning. This reduces the time and effort required to build models, enabling users with limited coding experience to develop high-quality AI solutions.

Another core feature is AutoTS (Automated Time Series), which helps organizations build models that can make predictions based on time-based data, such as forecasting sales or supply chain demands. MLOps (Machine Learning Operations) is also a critical component, providing tools to manage, monitor, and govern machine learning models in production environments. This ensures that models remain effective and up-to-date as business needs evolve.

DataRobot's platform is used across a variety of industries, including finance, healthcare, retail, manufacturing, and government. In finance, it helps banks and investment firms automate processes like fraud detection, risk assessment, and credit scoring. In healthcare, it is used to predict patient outcomes, optimize resource allocation, and assist in medical research. Retailers use it for customer segmentation, personalized marketing, and inventory optimization. Manufacturing companies leverage it to enhance predictive maintenance and optimize supply chain operations.

DataRobot is widely used by companies seeking to adopt AI-driven decision-making without needing large in-house AI teams. Data scientists and ML engineers use it to streamline the model-building process, while business analysts and executives use it for generating insights without extensive technical expertise. By democratizing access to AI, DataRobot empowers a broader range of employees to utilize machine learning tools.

The platform helps organizations improve operational

efficiency, reduce costs, and drive better decision-making. It also provides a robust governance framework to ensure that AI models are deployed responsibly and adhere to regulatory requirements. By automating the more technical aspects of AI development, DataRobot allows companies to focus on leveraging AI to solve specific business challenges.

## DeepSeek

**DeepSeek** is a Chinese artificial intelligence company that develops open-source large language models (LLMs).

The **DeepSeek-R1** model provides responses comparable to other contemporary LLMs, such as **OpenAI**'s **GPT-4o.** DeepSeek is an open-source large language model that relies on inference-time computing. The system activates only the most relevant portions of the model for each query, and as a result, requires a tenth of the computing power of a comparable LLM. In addition, DeepSeek-R1 can be trained at a significantly lower cost—$6 million compared to $100 million for OpenAI's GPT-4 in 2023.

## Google Cloud AI Platform

**Google Cloud AI Platform** is a comprehensive suite of machine learning (ML) and artificial intelligence (AI) products designed to help businesses, developers, and data scientists build, deploy, and manage AI models at scale. It provides a range of tools and services to streamline the process of creating AI-driven applications, from data preparation and model training to deployment and monitoring.

Google Cloud AI Platform offers managed **AI Jupyter Notebooks** that allow developers and data scientists to collaborate on machine learning tasks, such as data exploration, feature engineering, and model building, without worrying about infrastructure management.

Users can train machine learning models on Google's powerful infrastructure, using both CPUs and GPUs, with support for TensorFlow, PyTorch, and other popular ML frameworks. This service automatically handles scaling, resource management, and job monitoring, making large-scale training more efficient.

Once models are trained, **AI Platform Prediction** allows users to deploy them for serving real-time or batch predictions. The platform ensures that models are highly available, scalable, and optimized for latency, making it easier for businesses to integrate AI predictions into their applications.

A suite of Google AI services, including **AutoML Vision**, **AutoML Natural Language**, and **AutoML Tables**, enable users with limited machine learning expertise to build custom models by automating key processes like feature selection, algorithm tuning, and model training.

**Vertex AI** is the next-generation platform that unifies Google's AI services, making it easier to deploy and scale AI models. It integrates AutoML, model monitoring, and AI pipelines, allowing businesses to accelerate AI adoption with a streamlined, end-to-end workflow for building and operationalizing ML models.

Google Cloud AI provides pre-trained, ready-to-use APIs for tasks like speech-to-text, translation, and image recognition, which allow developers to integrate AI features into their applications without building models from scratch.

The platform is widely used by enterprises, startups, and academic institutions for various applications, including predictive analytics, customer service automation, healthcare diagnostics, fraud detection, and more. Businesses leverage Google Cloud AI to innovate faster and improved decision-making by incorporating AI into their products and processes, while data scientists and ML engineers use it for experimentation, research, and production-grade AI deployments.

## GROK

**Grok** is an AI assistant and chatbot developed by xAI, an artificial intelligence (AI) company founded by Elon Musk in 2023. Grok is able to generate text and images and engage in conversations with users, similar to ChatGPT and other tools. Unlike other chatbots, though, it can access information in real-time through the web and X (formerly Twitter), and is programmed to sometimes respond to edgy and provocative questions with witty and "rebellious" answers. Said one reviewer: "Grok 3 is not just another AI update.

It feels like a paradigm shift—a step toward a more intuitive, responsive, and unsettlingly human-like intelligence. It outpaces most competitors in speed, logic, and contextual depth. Yet, it's still an AI: powerful, impressive, but not quite sentient."[15]

## H2O AI

**H2O.ai** is a leading AI platform that offers cutting-edge machine learning and artificial intelligence solutions to organizations looking to optimize business processes through data-driven insights. The company is known for its open-source platform, **H2O**, and its enterprise-focused product suite, **H2O Driverless AI**, which enable businesses to develop, deploy, and manage AI models with ease and efficiency.

At the heart of H2O.ai's offerings is its open-source machine learning platform, H2O, which provides a wide range of algorithms for building predictive models. It supports common tasks such as classification, regression, clustering, and anomaly detection, making it suitable for a variety of applications.

This platform is designed to be highly scalable, capable of handling large datasets, and is integrated with popular data science tools like Python, R, and Spark. H2O's flexibility allows data scientists and developers to experiment with complex models and integrate them into business workflows seamlessly.

The company's flagship product, H2O Driverless AI, automates many aspects of the machine learning process, from data preparation and feature engineering to model building and hyperparameter tuning. This automated machine learning (AutoML) platform enables organizations to rapidly develop AI models without requiring deep expertise in data science. H2O Driverless AI uses advanced techniques like genetic algorithms and machine learning interpretability (MLI) to not only build accurate models but also explain their results, ensuring transparency and trust in AI-driven decision-making.

H2O.ai products are used by a wide range of industries, including finance, healthcare, retail, and manufacturing. In finance, companies use H2O.ai for fraud detection, credit scoring, and algorithmic trading. Healthcare organizations leverage the

---

[15] https://latenode.com/blog/grok-3-review

platform for predictive modeling in patient care, personalized treatment, and disease prediction. Retailers utilize H2O.ai for customer segmentation, demand forecasting, and personalized marketing strategies.

H2O.ai's user base includes data scientists, business analysts, and software engineers, as well as non-technical users who benefit from its easy-to-use AutoML tools. By enabling faster, more efficient AI model development, H2O.ai helps organizations innovate, reduce costs, and drive data-centric decision-making.

## IBM Watson

**IBM Watson** is a suite of enterprise-grade artificial intelligence (AI) products and services developed by IBM to help businesses harness AI for various applications. Watson offers solutions for industries like healthcare, finance, retail, and government, providing tools to automate processes, analyze data, and enhance decision-making. It became famous by beating human champion Ken Jennings in *Jeopardy*.

**Watson Assistant** is a conversational AI platform designed to create chatbots and virtual assistants. Businesses use Watson Assistant to improve customer service by automating inquiries, streamlining interactions, and providing personalized responses. It supports multi-channel integrations across web, mobile, and voice platforms.

**Watson Discovery**, an AI-powered search engine, helps users extract valuable insights from complex documents and large datasets. It leverages natural language processing (NLP) to understand and interpret unstructured data, enabling faster data retrieval, trend analysis, and decision-making in industries like legal, research, and finance.

**Watson Natural Language Processing** is a set of tools for analyzing and understanding human language. It is widely used for text classification, sentiment analysis, and content extraction in customer feedback analysis, social media monitoring, and legal document review. Content extraction involves crawling the web to identify URLs that may contain useful data and then extracting the relevant information from those sites. Sentiment analysis analyzes whether the extracted articles are positive, negative, or neutral about the subject of the article.

**Watson Health** is focused on the healthcare industry. It helps clinicians and researchers analyze medical data, diagnose diseases, and develop treatment plans. It has been used in oncology, drug discovery, and genomics, enabling more personalized care and reducing the time it takes to bring new drugs to market.

Next, **Watson Studio** is an integrated environment that enables data scientists to build and train AI models. This platform supports machine learning, deep learning, and data visualization, making it easier for teams to collaborate and develop AI solutions for predictive analytics, fraud detection, or supply chain optimization.

## Infosys Nia

**Nia** is an AI platform developed by Infosys to help enterprises automate processes, improve decision-making, and drive business efficiency. Nia leverages machine learning (ML), natural language processing (NLP), and deep learning to transform enterprise operations, enabling organizations to extract meaningful insights from data and optimize business processes.

Nia provides an intelligent data platform that allows businesses to manage, process, and analyze vast volumes of structured and unstructured data. It simplifies data integration from multiple sources and offers advanced analytic tools to uncover hidden patterns, trends, and actionable insights. Industries use **Nia Data** for predictive maintenance, risk assessment, and customer behavior analysis.

Designed to capture and digitize institutional knowledge, Nia helps businesses create a knowledge repository that can be used to inform decision-making. By automating knowledge extraction from documents, contracts, and reports, this tool ensures that critical business information is always accessible. This is especially beneficial in industries like legal, finance, and healthcare, where large amounts of documentation must be analyzed and utilized.

Nia also gives you a suite of automation tools that focus on improving operational efficiency. **Nia Automation** enables robotic process automation (RPA) by automating repetitive tasks such as data entry, invoice processing, and customer support. This service helps businesses save time, reduce errors, and streamline workflows, particularly in finance, human resources, and supply chain management.

An AI-driven **Nia Chatbot** helps businesses to create virtual assistants for customer service and employee support. The Nia Chatbot leverages NLP to understand customer inquiries, resolve issues, and provide personalized responses across various channels like web, mobile, and social media.

## Jasper

**Jasper** is an AI-powered content creation platform designed to help individuals and businesses generate high-quality written content quickly and efficiently. Jasper leverages natural language processing (NLP) and machine learning to assist users in crafting a wide variety of content, including blog posts, marketing copy, social media updates, emails, and more. Jasper is particularly valuable for those who need to produce large volumes of content while maintaining a consistent tone, style, and quality.

One of Jasper's key features is its ability to generate text based on user prompts. By providing a few details, users can receive well-written drafts in seconds, significantly speeding up the content creation process. Jasper can assist with various types of writing, such as SEO-optimized blog posts, product descriptions, ad copy, newsletters, and creative storytelling. Its versatility and ability to adapt to different writing styles make it a popular choice for content marketers, copywriters, and social media managers.

Jasper also includes tools for long-form content creation, making it useful for authors and bloggers who want to develop in-depth articles or eBooks. With its AI-driven capabilities, users can outline, write, and edit long-form content in a fraction of the time it would take manually. Additionally, the platform offers templates and workflows to streamline the creation of different content types, such as persuasive emails or engaging social media captions.

Beyond writing, Jasper can assist with brainstorming and idea generation. It helps users overcome writer's block by suggesting topics, headlines, or even entire paragraphs based on the context provided. Jasper's ability to generate ideas and structure content is especially useful for those in creative roles, like content strategists and marketers.

## Jupyter Notebooks

**Jupyter Notebooks** is an open-source web-based tool designed for interactive computing, primarily used in the fields of data science, machine learning, artificial intelligence (AI), and academic research. It allows users to create and share documents that combine live code, equations, visualizations, and narrative text in a single environment. Its name, Jupyter, is derived from three core programming languages—Julia, Python, and R—though it supports over 40 languages in total, making it a highly versatile tool.

In AI and data science, Jupyter Notebooks is popular for exploratory data analysis (EDA), model development, and testing. Users can write Python code to manipulate data, implement machine learning algorithms, and visualize the results without needing to switch between different software environments. This flexibility makes it a favorite among AI engineers, data scientists, and academic researchers who require a fast and interactive platform for prototyping machine learning models or analyzing datasets.

The platform is especially useful in collaborative environments. Teams working on AI projects can share their notebooks through platforms like GitHub or **JupyterHub**, allowing others to review, edit, and run the code. This facilitates better collaboration in educational settings, research institutions, and industry AI projects, where reproducibility and transparency are critical.

Jupyter's ability to integrate with powerful AI libraries like TensorFlow, PyTorch, and Scikit-learn enhances its appeal among machine learning practitioners. It also supports visualization tools such as Matplotlib, Plotly, and Seaborn, making it easier to plot data and observe trends.

AI students and instructors use Jupyter Notebooks for teaching purposes, as it enables them to demonstrate concepts with live examples that students can directly manipulate. Additionally, business analysts and AI developers use it for presenting AI-driven insights or reports to stakeholders, combining code output with explanatory text and visualizations in one cohesive document.

## Observe.ai

**Observe.ai** is an AI-powered platform that enhances customer experience by analyzing, optimizing, and automating customer interactions, particularly in contact centers. Its core services include conversational intelligence, quality assurance, and agent performance management. By leveraging artificial intelligence, the platform transforms unstructured voice and text interactions into actionable insights, helping businesses improve customer service, operational efficiency, and agent performance.

One of Observe.ai's key offerings is its conversational intelligence feature. This tool automatically transcribes and analyzes customer interactions in real-time or after the fact, identifying patterns, sentiment, keywords, and topics within conversations. It applies natural language processing (NLP) and machine learning algorithms to interpret the data, uncovering valuable insights about customer behavior and preferences. This allows companies to fine-tune their support strategies, improve agent training, and better meet customer needs.

In addition, Observe.ai's quality assurance (QA) solution automates the process of evaluating agent performance. Traditionally, QA teams would manually review a small percentage of customer calls to ensure compliance and service quality. With Observe.ai, 100% of interactions are analyzed, making it possible to detect and address issues like policy violations or missed sales opportunities more comprehensively. The AI-powered system can flag key moments in conversations, ensuring adherence to compliance standards and identifying areas for improvement.

In addition, Observe.ai provides agents with real-time coaching and feedback based on their conversations, helping them improve customer interactions dynamically. With the detailed insights generated by the AI, managers can deliver personalized training to each agent, addressing their specific areas of growth, and encouraging better performance overall.

Observe.ai is primarily used by businesses with large-scale customer support operations, including contact centers across industries like telecommunications, financial services, healthcare, and e-commerce.

## Salesforce Einstein

**Salesforce Einstein**, an AI-driven platform integrated into **Salesforce's Customer Relationship Management** (CRM) suite, helps businesses automate tasks, gain predictive insights, and make smarter decisions based on customer data. It provides AI functionalities like predictive analytics, natural language processing (NLP), and machine learning (ML) to enhance various aspects of customer relationship management. Key features include:

**Einstein Analytics** offers deep data insights by automating data preparation and visualization, allowing users to monitor key performance indicators (KPIs) and uncover trends from vast datasets. It helps sales, marketing, and service teams identify opportunities and risks, enabling data-driven decision-making. For example, sales teams can predict which leads are most likely to convert, while marketing teams can segment audiences based on predictive behaviors.

**Einstein Prediction Builder** allows users to create custom AI models tailored to their business needs, without needing to write complex code. This enables companies to predict outcomes like customer churn, product returns, or lifetime value, helping teams take proactive actions to retain customers or boost revenue.

**Einstein Discovery** applies machine learning to uncover hidden patterns and make recommendations. It automates the process of analyzing large datasets to explain why certain outcomes are happening and suggests actions to improve business results. This can help companies optimize processes like sales pipelines, customer service operations, and marketing campaigns.

**Einstein Bots** use natural language processing to power intelligent chatbots that handle routine customer inquiries, reducing the workload on support teams. These bots can be integrated into websites or mobile apps to assist customers in real-time, providing immediate answers or escalating more complex issues to human agents.

**Salesforce Einstein** is primarily used by sales, marketing, and customer service teams across industries such as retail, finance, healthcare, and technology. It enables businesses to streamline processes, improve customer experiences, and make data-driven decisions, enhancing overall business performance with the power of AI; examples include **Siri** and **Alexa**.

## TensorFlow

**TensorFlow** is an open-source machine learning platform developed by Google, widely used for building and deploying AI applications. It provides a comprehensive ecosystem for developing machine learning models, particularly for tasks involving deep learning and neural networks. TensorFlow is designed to handle both the research and production phases of machine learning, enabling developers to go from experimentation to deployment in a streamlined way.

One of the core features of TensorFlow is its support for deep learning, where neural networks with many layers are trained on vast amounts of data to solve complex tasks like image recognition, natural language processing, and speech recognition. TensorFlow allows users to build these neural networks with flexible tools that support different levels of abstraction, from high-level APIs (like Keras) for quick model prototyping to low-level APIs for fine-tuning.

TensorFlow's versatility also makes it suitable for both small-scale machine learning tasks and large-scale distributed computations. It supports multiple environments, from running on a single device (such as a mobile phone) to utilizing cloud infrastructure and large-scale distributed systems. This flexibility enables enterprises to more easily scale their machine learning models.

A lightweight version of the system, **TensorFlow Lite**, is designed for deploying machine learning models on mobile and embedded devices. It allows developers to bring AI capabilities to edge devices like smartphones, IoT gadgets, and smart cameras, enabling real-time inference with minimal computational resources.

## Tractable

**Tractable** develops AI solutions for visual damage assessment, particularly in the insurance, automotive, and disaster recovery sectors. Their products use computer vision to analyze images and videos, enabling businesses to assess damage more quickly, accurately, and cost-effectively. This streamlines processes like claims management, vehicle repair estimates, and disaster recovery, reducing manual work and speeding up resolution times.

The company's flagship product, **AI Estimating**, focuses on vehicle damage assessment. By using computer vision to analyze photos of damaged vehicles, the AI can generate repair estimates in minutes. This technology enables insurers, repair shops, and automotive companies to quickly determine the extent of damage, required repairs, and associated costs.

What's more, it reduces the need for physical inspections, which can be time-consuming and costly, allowing claims to be processed faster, often within hours of an accident. Tractable's AI Estimating tool integrates seamlessly into existing workflows, making it easy for businesses to adopt without major operational changes.

Another key offering is **AI Property**, which focuses on damage assessment for homes and buildings, particularly in the aftermath of natural disasters such as hurricanes or floods. The AI analyzes photos of property damage, helping insurers and property owners quickly understand the extent of the damage and what repairs are necessary. This is especially valuable in large-scale disaster scenarios where immediate assessments are critical to recovery efforts.

## Viso Suite

**Viso Suite** is a no-code platform for building, deploying, and managing computer vision applications. It is designed to enable businesses and developers to harness the power of AI-driven visual data analysis without the need for extensive programming skills. Viso Suite provides a unified environment that covers the entire lifecycle of AI vision projects, from creating models and integrating them with real-time video streams to deployment and monitoring across multiple devices.

Viso Suite allows users to design and customize AI models for tasks like object detection, tracking, facial recognition, and anomaly detection. Its interface simplifies complex workflows, making AI accessible to non-experts while still offering the flexibility that experienced developers need for fine-tuning. Viso Suite supports integration with various hardware, from IoT devices to edge servers, enabling AI deployment across industries.

Viso Suite is highly scalable and can be used in small pilots or large-scale deployments with thousands of cameras or edge devices. It also facilitates cloud and edge computing, offering the flexibility to run AI models locally for faster real-time processing or in the cloud for centralized data management.

This platform is used by a wide range of industries, including retail, manufacturing, healthcare, logistics, and smart cities. In retail, for instance, AI models can be applied for analyzing customer behavior, tracking store traffic, and preventing shoplifting. In manufacturing, Viso Suite is used for quality control and predictive maintenance, detecting defects or irregularities in products. Smart cities leverage the platform for traffic management and public safety through video surveillance systems.

# Glossary

- **Activation Function**: A function used in neural networks to introduce non-linearity into the model, helping it to learn complex patterns. Examples include ReLU (Rectified Linear Unit) and sigmoid functions.
- **Algorithm**: A step-by-step procedure or formula for solving a problem. In AI, algorithms are used to process data, train models, and make predictions.
- **Artificial Intelligence (AI)**: The simulation of human intelligence processes by machines, especially computer systems. This includes learning, reasoning, and self-correction.
- **Bias**: A systematic error introduced by an algorithm or model that leads to skewed or unfair results, often due to biased training data or model design.
- **Computer Vision**: An AI field that enables machines to interpret and make decisions based on visual inputs from the world, such as images or videos.
- **Deep Learning**: A branch of machine learning that uses neural networks with many layers (deep neural networks) to model complex patterns in large datasets.
- **Explainable AI (XAI)**: An area of AI focused on creating models and systems whose decisions and processes can be understood and interpreted by humans, increasing transparency and trust.
- **F1 Score**: A metric that combines precision and recall into a single score, providing a balance between the two. It is the harmonic mean of precision and recall.

- **Feature**: An individual measurable property or characteristic of a phenomenon being observed, used as input for machine learning models.
- **Generative Adversarial Network (GAN)**: A type of neural network architecture consisting of two networks, a generator and a discriminator, that are trained together to generate new, synthetic data that resembles real data.
- **Label**: The output or target value that a machine learning model is trying to predict or classify, often used in supervised learning.
- **Large language model (LLM).** A type of artificial intelligence (AI) program that can analyze and understand text. LLMs are trained on massive amounts of data, such as books and articles, to learn how language works. They are built on a type of neural network called a transformer model.
- **Machine Learning (ML)**: A subset of AI that involves training algorithms to learn from and make predictions or decisions based on data.
- **Natural Language Processing (NLP)**: A field of AI focused on the interaction between computers and humans through natural language, enabling machines to understand, interpret, and respond to human language.
- **Neural Network**: A computational model inspired by the human brain's network of neurons. It consists of interconnected nodes (neurons) that process information in layers. Those with the largest number of interconnected nodes are called deep neural networks.
- **Open Source**. A type of software or project where the source code is made freely available for anyone to view, modify, and distribute. Unlike proprietary software, where the code is restricted and owned by a company or individual, open-source software encourages collaboration and transparency.
- **Overfitting**: A modeling error that occurs when a machine learning model learns the training data too well, capturing noise and outliers rather than general patterns, leading to poor performance on new data.

- **Precision**: A measure of a model's accuracy in identifying true positives among all positive predictions, calculated as the ratio of true positives to the sum of true and false positives.
- **Recall**: A measure of a model's ability to identify all relevant instances in the dataset, calculated as the ratio of true positives to the sum of true positives and false negatives.
- **Reinforcement Learning**: A type of machine learning where an agent learns to make decisions by taking actions in an environment to maximize cumulative rewards.
- **Supervised Learning**: A type of machine learning where the model is trained on labeled data, meaning each training example is paired with an output label.
- **Test Data**: The dataset used to evaluate the final performance of a machine learning model, ensuring that it generalizes well to new, unseen data.
- **Training Data**: The dataset used to train a machine learning model, which includes both input features and the corresponding output labels.
- **Transfer Learning**: A machine learning technique where a model developed for one task is reused or adapted for a different but related task, leveraging previously learned knowledge.
- **Underfitting**: A situation where a machine learning model is too simple to capture the underlying patterns in the data, resulting in poor performance on both training and new data.
- **Unsupervised Learning**: A type of machine learning where the model is trained on unlabeled data, and it tries to identify patterns or structures in the data without predefined labels.
- **Validation Data**: A separate dataset used to tune the model's parameters and evaluate its performance during training, helping to prevent overfitting.

# Bibliography


Bly, Robert, *The Science Fictionary* (Crystal Lake, 2023).

Broderick, Damien and Paul Di Filippo, *Science Fiction: the 101 Best Novels 1985-2010* (Nonstop Press, 2012).

Luciano, Patrick and Gary Coville, *American Science Fiction Television Series of the 1950s* (McFarland, 2007).

Warren, Bill, *Keep Watching the Skies* (McFarland, 2000).

# Acknowledgements

Thanks to Joe Mynhardt at Crystal Lake Publishing for his patience and understanding, and for publishing this book. David McCoy gets credit for the fun and accurate illustrations. And thanks to Jennifer Holmes for her contributions to the text.

# About the Author

Robert W. Bly is a freelance writer who has written more than 100 books including *The Science Fictionary* (Crystal Lake) and *Freak Show of the Gods* (Quill Driver).

Bob's articles have appeared in *Cosmopolitan, City Paper, Writer's Digest, New Jersey Monthly*, and many other publications. He has written sales and technical materials for dozens of companies including IBM, AT&T, Network Solutions, and BOC Gases.

Bly holds a B.S in chemical engineering from the University of Rochester and is a member of the American Institute of Chemical Engineers. He is also trained as a certified Novell NetWare Administrator.

His copywriting website is www.bly.com and his science fiction site is www.sciencefictionprediction.com.

Readers . . .

Thank you for reading *AI Apocalypse*. We hope you enjoyed this reference guide.

If you have a moment, please review *AI Apocalypse* at the store where you bought it.

Help other readers by telling them why you enjoyed this book. No need to write an in-depth discussion. Even a single sentence will be greatly appreciated. Reviews go a long way to helping a book sell, and is great for an author's career. It'll also help us to continue publishing quality books.

Thank you again for taking the time to journey with Crystal Lake Publishing.

Visit our Linktree page for a list of our social media platforms.
https://linktr.ee/CrystalLakePublishing

**Follow us on Amazon:**

# MISSION STATEMENT:

Since its founding in August 2012, Crystal Lake has quickly become one of the world's leading publishers of Dark Fiction and Horror books. In 2023, Crystal Lake officially transitioned into an entertainment company, joining several other divisions, genres, and imprints, including Torrid Waters, Sinister Smile Press, Crystal Lake Comics, Crystal Lake Games, Crystal Cove Press, Crystal Lake Kids, Memento Mori Ink, and The House of Shadows & Ink on YouTube.

While we strive to present only the highest quality fiction and entertainment, we also endeavor to support authors along their writing journey. We offer our time and experience in non-fiction projects, as well as author mentoring and services, at competitive prices.

With several Bram Stoker Award wins and many other wins and nominations (including the HWA's Specialty Press Award), Crystal Lake puts integrity, honor, and respect at the forefront of our publishing operations.

We strive for each book and outreach program we spearhead to not only entertain and touch or comment on issues that affect our readers, but also to strengthen and support the Dark Fiction field and its authors.

Not only do we find and publish authors we believe are destined for greatness, but we strive to work with men and women who endeavor to be decent human beings who care more for others than themselves, while still being hard-working, driven, and passionate artists and storytellers.

Crystal Lake is and will always be a beacon of what passion and dedication, combined with overwhelming teamwork and respect, can accomplish. We endeavor to know each and every one of our readers, while building personal relationships with our authors, reviewers, bloggers, podcasters, bookstores, and libraries.

We will be as trustworthy, forthright, and transparent as any business can be, while also keeping most of the headaches away from our authors, since it's our job to solve the problems so they can stay in a creative mind. Which of course also means paying our authors.

We do not just publish books, we present to you worlds within your world, doors within your mind, from talented authors who sacrifice so much for a moment of your time.

There are some amazing small presses out there, and through collaboration and open forums we will continue to support other presses in the goal of helping authors and showing the world what quality small presses are capable of accomplishing. No one wins when a small press goes down, so we will always be there to support hardworking, legitimate presses and their authors. We don't see Crystal Lake as the best press out there, but we will always strive to be the best, strive to be the most interactive and grateful, and even blessed press around. No matter what happens over time, we will also take our mission very seriously while appreciating where we are and enjoying the journey.

What do we offer our authors that they can't do for themselves through self-publishing?

We are big supporters of self-publishing (especially hybrid publishing), if done with care, patience, and planning. However, not every author has the time or inclination to do market research, advertise, and set up book launch strategies. Although a lot of authors are successful in doing it all, strong small presses will always be there for the authors who just want to do what they do best: write.

What we offer is experience, industry knowledge, contacts and trust built up over years. And due to our strong brand and trusting fanbase, every Crystal Lake book comes with weight of respect. In time our fans begin to trust our judgment and will try a new author purely based on our support of said author.

To date we've published around 300 books, and with each launch we strive to fine-tune our approach, learn from our mistakes, and increase our reach. We continue to assure our authors that we're here for them and that we'll carry the weight of the launch and deal with third parties while they focus on their strengths—be it writing, interviews, blogs, signings, etc.

We also offer several mentoring packages to authors that include knowledge and skills they can use in both traditional and self-publishing endeavors. This includes Shadows & Ink Creators on our The House of Shadows & Ink YouTube channel and our Crystal Lake Academy.

We look forward to launching many new careers.

This is what we believe in. What we stand for. This will be our legacy.

**Welcome to Crystal Lake Publishing—**
**Where stories come alive!**

www.ingramcontent.com/pod-product-compliance
Lightning Source LLC
Chambersburg PA
CBHW022050020426
42335CB00012B/618
* 9 7 8 1 9 6 8 5 3 2 4 0 6 *